TIBETAN FOLK TALES

TIBETAN
FOLK TALES

Fredrick and Audrey Hyde-Chambers

Illustrated by Kusho Ralla

SHAMBHALA
BOSTON & LONDON
2001

SHAMBHALA PUBLICATIONS, INC.
Horticultural Hall
300 Massachusetts Avenue
Boston, Massachusetts 02115
www.shambhala.com

Printed in the United States of America

⊗ This edition is printed on acid-free paper that meets the American
National Standards Institute z39.48 Standard.
Distributed in the United States by Random House, Inc., and in Canada
by Random House of Canada Ltd

The Library of Congress catalogs the previous edition of this
title as follows:
Hyde-Chambers, Fredrick.
Tibetan folk tales.
Summary: A collection of folk-tales from one of the last ancient
civilizations to be explored by the West.
1. Tales—Tibet [1. Folklore—Tibet]   I. Hyde-Chambers, Audrey
II. Kusho Ralla, illustrator. III. Title.
PZ8.1.H998Ti   398.2'09515   81-50970
ISBN 1-57062-090-3 (pbk.)
ISBN 1-57062-892-0 (pbk.)

CONTENTS

This life, you must know as the tiny
    splash of a raindrop,
A thing of beauty that disappears even
    as it comes into being.

Therefore, set your goal.
Make use of every day and night
    to achieve it.

—Tsongkhapa

INTRODUCTION

An ancient poem describes Tibet as "the center of high snow mountains, the source of great rivers; a lofty country, a pure land." It is an accurate description: the average altitude of Tibet is 16,000 feet and the country is surrounded by the world's highest mountain ranges—the Kunlun on the North, the Karakoram and Ladakh mountains on the West, and the Himalayas on the South and East. Waters flow from prehistoric glaciers in Tibet to form the Indus, Sutlej, Brahmaputra, Salween, Mekong, and Yangtze rivers.

Tibet was the last of the old civilizations, a repository of much that was believed lost with the passing of ancient Egypt, Persia, and India. "The Land of Snow" has been called the most religious country in the world, seen by some as a land of worldly saints, and by others as a land oppressed by superstition. Neither view is quite exact: Tibet was unusual because the guiding principles of its society were spiritual values. Tibetans widely acknowledged the importance of those values and, as the stories collected here demonstrate, they pervaded all aspects of life.

The preeminence of the spiritual, however, was balanced by the characteristic Tibetan sense of humor and love of commerce. Tibetans seem to be born merchants; their travels in pursuit of trade are equal to Marco Polo's. Their sense of humor, especially evident in those who seriously undertake the spiritual life, is widely recognized by Westerners who have worked with Tibetan refugees who often tell the most harrowing stories of their escapes while joking about experiences that might easily have left them deeply embittered.

In 1959 the last vestiges of free Tibet vanished when a national uprising was crushed by the Chinese. As a result, thousands of Tibetans, including the Dalai Lama (the spiritual and temporal leader of Tibet), undertook an astonishing journey to seek refuge in India. There are now 100,000 Tibetan refugees there and in Nepal and Bhutan. While they have adapted themselves to new environments, the refugees have also sought not only to preserve but also to live their traditional inheritance, but it is inevitable that much of it will be lost. In Tibet storytelling was one of the most popular forms of family entertainment, and good storytellers were in great demand. As a Tibetan friend told us, "Storytelling was our television." So we hope that we, too, will entertain our readers with these myths and stories while presenting a little of the richness of Tibetan culture.

Almost all Tibetan folk tales are set in Tibet, which allows the storyteller to leave a lot to his audience's imagination. We have tried to fill in the Tibetan background in the stories; some fuller explanations of Tibetan customs will be found in the Notes. The Tibetan attitude toward fantastic events, such as those recounted in the epic of Gesar, has caused some readers to think them gullible. Tibetans, for their part, are very surprised that we can so confidently regard our everyday world as immutable reality, especially when no two people can possibly see the same thing in the same way. In Tibetan Buddhist philosophy, the way we perceive reality is compared to a sleeping man who has every belief in his dream. This view is traditionally illustrated by a verse from the Prajnaparamita literature:

> All created forms are like a mirage,
> Like clouds in the sky,
> Like images in a dream;
> Thus must all things be regarded.

Some of the stories collected here have very ancient origins; they have been handed down through generations of storytellers. In traditional societies storytelling is regarded as a considerable responsibility and storytellers have carefully trained memories. Generations of Tibetan lamas have given special oral instructions on the use of particular religious texts. Monks also participated in dialectical debates in which they would make word-perfect quotations of extensive passages from the religious literature. Thus, the art of memorization was important in the training of monks and the oral tradition was vital in preserving both cultural and religious information.

The legends and folk tales we have included in this collection are mostly from firsthand sources, especially Yeshe Tsultim and Kusho Ralla. Yeshe Tsultim has a remarkable fund of Tibetan folk tales which he learned from his mother who was a great story-teller. He was born forty-four years ago on the Sino-Tibetan border in Kham, East Tibet, and began his studies when he entered the Tharlom Drami Gonpa monastery at the age of six. Some years later he went to Lhasa, the Tibetan capital, to enroll at Gyuto monastery. His religious training has clearly been carefully balanced with practical skills. Currently he is warden of one of the Ockenden Venture Homes for Vietnamese refugees in England.

Kusho Ralla was also born in Kham, East Tibet, forty-six years ago. He is recognized as the thirteenth incarnation or "tulku" of Ra lotsawa, a Tibetan spiritual teacher. When he was seven Kusho Ralla began studies at his namesake's monastery of Samdo and he eventually took his degree at the Sera monastic university in Lhasa. He was trained in the traditional Tibetan method of painting thangkas, the religious scroll paintings which are used for meditation and which are painted in a very definite style. He is almost certainly unique among the few artists who managed to escape from Tibet in his ability to translate his native artistic tradition into effective modern book illustration.

A Note on Tibetan Buddhism

Buddhism was first brought to Tibet in the eighth century A.D. by the Indian guru Padmasambhava, and was later established by King Songtsen Gampo who was converted to the faith by his Chinese and Nepalese wives. The teachings of the Buddha, based on wisdom and compassion, became an integral part of the life of the Tibetan people. The ordinary people, not versed in scholastic interpretation, practiced their faith from the heart. Everyday household items were decorated with sacred symbols. Prayer flags (strips of cloth printed with prayers) fluttered from tall poles or were hung from trees and rooftops throughout the land. Prayer wheels, hollow containers mounted on spindles, were filled with sacred texts and decorated on the outside with prayers. They were turned by hand, driven by water from rivers or streams, or rotated by warm air from lamps; each revolution was an invocation and a reminder of the national religion.

For the Tibetan people, faith is not a blind acceptance of a divine being outside of oneself, but rather a dynamic determination, an unshakeable belief in the ability of all beings to attain enlightenment. Tibetans believe it is only our false view of reality that prevents us from becoming enlightened. As if there were a veil clouding our vision, our perceptions are disturbed by ignorance, greed, hate, and delusion. Enlightenment, if it can be described at all, is like awakening from a dream. It is to see the universe "as it is," to experience the harmony of life, to be free from our concepts, biases, and opinions.

All the gods, deities, demons, and other beings in Tibetan iconography are aspects of the many-faceted personality of man. A diamond is a diamond, yet it has many facets; a man is a man, but with many sides to his personality. Just as a diamond reflects its surroundings, so man reflects enlightenment. Tibetans view all life as sacred since all beings—gods, humans, animals, or insects—are considered as parts of the whole.

The historical Buddha Gautama was born the son of a ruler in Kapilavastu, the city of the Shakya clan in the Kathmandu valley, some five hundred fifty years before Christ. Disillusioned with worldly life, he left his home to become a wandering ascetic. He sought out great Indian gurus as teachers and practiced all their instructions, which ranged from atheism to methods of mind and body control that often involved extremes of indulgence or rigorous self-discipline. Still Gautama was not satisfied. He sought to know the real nature of existence, the truth about birth, disease, old age, and death. He gave up the ascetic life, took some food to restore the strength drained by his severe practices, sat down under a tree and vowed not to move until he had discovered the truth. In the night of his enlightenment, many temptations invaded his mind, but he remained firm in his resolve and finally discovered the truth, the real nature of existence.

At first the Buddha ("Awakened One") only taught a few close followers, but later he was persuaded to make his teaching more widely known. He delivered his first sermon, "Turning the Wheel of Dharma," at the Deer Park in Benares. In it he set forth the "four noble truths" of suffering, its cause, its end, and the way to that end, which form the foundation of Buddhist belief. The two golden deer supporting a wheel which appear above the entrances of Tibetan temples are memorials of that first sermon.

Although Tibetan Buddhism holds that all beings are capable of enlightenment, enlightenment is not the end of the path, for the ultimate goal is to lead all beings to that attainment. For this reason the potential buddha renounces enlightenment for himself and returns to the world to teach until all beings are liberated. This is known as the "bodhisattva ideal." A bodhisattva is a "wisdom being;" of the many bodhisattvas who figure in Tibetan Buddhism, Chenrezik, the Lord of Compassion, is the most revered.

THE CREATION

I N THE BEGINNING WAS VOIDNESS, a vast emptiness without cause, without end. From this great voidness there arose gentle stirrings of wind, which after countless eons grew thicker and heavier, forming the mighty double thunderbolt scepter Dorje Gyatram.

Dorje Gyatram created the clouds, which in turn created the rain. The rain fell for many years until the primeval ocean Gyatso was formed. Then, all was calm, quiet, and peaceful; the ocean became clear as a mirror.

Slowly the winds began to breathe once more, gently moving over the waters of the ocean, churning them continually until a light foam appeared on the surface. Just as cream is churned into butter, so were the waters of Gyatso churned into earth by the rhythmic motion of the winds.

The earth rose like a mountain, and around its peaks murmured the wind, ever moving, tireless, forming cloud upon cloud from which fell more rain, only this time heavier and full of salt, giving birth to the great oceans of the universe.

The center of the universe is Rirap Lhunpo (Sumeru) the great four-sided mountain made of precious stones and full of beautiful things. There are rivers and streams on Rirap Lhunpo and many kinds of trees, fruits, and plants, for Rirap Lhunpo is special—it is the abode of the gods and demi-gods.

Around Rirap Lhunpo is a great lake, and encircling the lake a ring of golden mountains. Beyond the ring of golden

1

mountains is another lake, it too encircled by mountains of gold, and so on, seven lakes, seven rings of golden mountains, and outside the last ring of mountains is the lake Chi Gyatso.

It is in Chi Gyatso that the four worlds are found, each like an island, with its own particular shape and distinct inhabitants. The world of the East is Lu Phak and is shaped like the half moon. People of Lu Phak live for five hundred years and they are peaceful; there is no fighting in Lu Phak. The people have bodies like giants and faces shaped like the half moon. They are not as fortunate as us, however, for they have no religion to follow.

The western world is called Balang Cho and is like the sun in shape. As in Lu Phak the people are large and live for five hundred years, but they have faces shaped like the sun and they keep many kinds of cattle.

The land of the North is square in shape and is called Dra Mi Nyen. People of Dra Mi Nyen have square faces and they live for a thousand years or more. In Dra Mi Nyen food and riches are abundant. Everything a man needs in his thousand-year lifetime comes to him without effort or suffering—he lives in luxury, wanting for nothing. But during the last seven days of life pain and mental torture attack the beings of Dra Mi Nyen, for then they receive a sign that they are about to die. A voice comes and whispers to them—a terrible voice—saying how they will die and what monstrous suffering they will endure in the hells after death. In the last seven days of life all their riches and possessions decay and they endure more suffering than we experience in a lifetime. Dra Mi Nyen is known as "The Land of the Fearful Voice."

Our own world in the South is called Dzambu Ling. At first our world was inhabited by gods from Rirap Lhunpo. There was no pain or sickness, nor did the gods ever want for food. They lived in contentment, spending their days in deep meditation. There was no need for light on Dzambu Ling then, for the gods emitted a pure light from their own bodies.

One day one of the gods noticed that on the surface of the earth there was a cream-like substance, and tasting it he found it to be delightful to the palate and encouraged the other gods to taste it. All the gods so enjoyed eating the creamy food that they would eat nothing else, and the more they ate the more their powers diminished. No longer were they able to sit in deep meditation; the light that once shone so brightly from their bodies began to fade, and finally was lost altogether. The world was clothed in darkness, and the mighty gods of Rirap Lhunpo became human beings.

Then, out of the darkness of night there appeared in the heavens the sun, and when the sun faded the moon and stars lit up the sky and illumined the world. The sun, moon, and stars appeared because of the past good deeds of the gods, and are a constant reminder to us that our world was once a peaceful, beautiful place, free from grasping, suffering, and pain.

When the people of Dzambu Ling had exhausted the supply of creamy food, they began to eat the fruit of the nyugu plant. Each person had his own plant, which produced a corn-like fruit, and each day, as one fruit was eaten, another would appear, one a day, which was enough to satisfy the hunger of the beings of Dzambu Ling.

One morning a man awoke to find that instead of producing only a single fruit his plant had grown two. Feeling greedy, he ate the two fruits, but the next day his plant was empty. Needing to satisfy his hunger, the man stole someone else's plant, and so it went on and on, each person needing to steal from another in order to eat. With theft came greed, and each person, afraid of being left without, began to grow more and more nyugu plants, having to work harder and harder to ensure that he would have enough to eat.

Strange things began to happen on Dzambu Ling. What used to be the peaceful abode of gods from Rirap Lhunpo was now full of men who knew theft and greed. One day, a man felt that his genitals were causing him discomfort and tore them from his body, and so became a woman. This woman had contact with men and soon had children, who in turn had more children, and in a short time Dzambu Ling was filled with people, all of whom had to find food and places to live.

3

The people of Dzambu Ling did not live in peace together. There was much fighting and stealing; indeed, the people of our world began to experience real suffering arising from the unsatisfactory state in which they found themselves. The people knew that in order to survive they would have to become organized. They all gathered together and decided to elect a leader of the people, whom they called Mang Kur, meaning "many people made him king." Mang Kur taught the people to live in relative harmony, each with his own land on which to build a home and grow food.

This is how our world came to be, how from gods we became human beings, subject to disease, old age, and death. When we look into the night sky, or bask in the warm brilliance of the sun, we should remember that, but for the good deeds of the gods from the precious mountain of Rirap Lhunpo, we would be living in total darkness, and but for the greed and desire of one person our world would not know the suffering it experiences today.

As long as any living being
draws breath,
Wherever he shall be,
There, in compassion
Will the Buddha appear,
incarnate.

—*Ngon tok gyen*

NOTE: Compare Genesis: "In the beginning God created the heaven and the earth. And the earth was without form, and void; and darkness was upon the face of the deep. And the spirit of God moved upon the face of the waters."

OPAME, CHENREZIK, AND DOLMA

THE CELESTIAL BUDDHA OPAME (Amitabha) looked down on the world from his Pure Land, and saw the suffering of all beings. Opame felt great compassion for them. From this thought of compassion Chenrezik (Avalokiteshvara) was born: the embodiment of compassion, the Lord of Compassion. The mountains opened, and water poured forth over the land and flowed into the Indian Ocean. Chenrezik appeared on an island in the middle of Lhasa, and seeing the suffering of all beings, vowed that he would help all beings to realize nirvana, the ultimate reality, peace. Chenrezik vowed that he would never withdraw from the world until all living beings, right down to the last blade of grass, attained to peace.

In the lake there were many beings, and they all cried out for bodies. Chenrezik, hearing their cries, gave the beings the bodies that they asked for, but they were all the same, and so the beings all begged to be different from one another. Chenrezik then gave each of them a different body, each distinctive and unlike any other.

Chenrezik, the Lord of Compassion, preached the dharma, the teachings of the buddhas, that all beings in the lake, countless numbers of them, could attain nirvana. Many beings did attain the peace of nirvana, but everytime Chenrezik returned to the lake, there were many more beings, far more than he had already helped. Again Chenrezik preached the dharma, and again many beings attained nirvana.

When Chenrezik looked into the lake for the third time and saw so many beings needing help, he grew full of despair. Realizing what an impossible task he had set himself, he cried to the Celestial Buddha Opame that he wanted to give back his noble vow, for the task was too great for him alone to fulfill. In his despair and compassion Chenrezik's body shattered into innumerable pieces.

Opame, seeing his plight, reformed his body, giving him even more power to help all living beings. Chenrezik now had eleven heads, surmounted by Opame's own head, and a thousand arms, and an all-seeing eye in the palm of each hand. Still Chenrezik saw his task as impossible: even with a thousand arms and eleven heads, there were so many beings and their minds were so clouded with impure thoughts. Chenrezik cried, and from a crystal teardrop on his cheek, Dolma (Tara) was born to help him.

So there is not a being, no matter how insignificant, whose suffering is not seen by Chenrezik or by Dolma, and who cannot be touched by their compassion.

NOTE: The birth of Dolma was first told to us by a Western Buddhist scholar, and later authenticized by a native Tibetan. It is an example of the balance of male and female energies central to Tibetan Buddhist religion and literature. Regarding the vow, in Tibetan Buddhism vows that prove too difficult for one to keep may be returned.

THE BLOSSOM TREE

AT THE TIME OF THE BUDDHA, Benares had been the holy city of India for many centuries, and Hinduism was its ancient religion. The city was famous for fine temples, many built in beautiful leafy parks with pools of clear, undisturbed water, while the streets of Benares were full of jostling people going about their business, for trading had brought the city much wealth. Merchants had built themselves magnificent houses, and had furnished them with goods they acquired on their commercial travels.

In many ways Benares was like any city in the world today, for then, as now, men sought happiness in making money and in a multitude of other good and evil ways, while some searched for happiness in religious creeds or philosophical paths. Leaders of many new teachings came to Benares, among them the Buddha.

It happened that one day a wealthy merchant was checking the harness of his horse in the courtyard of one of the larger houses, while shouting men and women strapped packs onto the wooden saddles of braying mules, their constantly moving feet kicking up clouds of dust. A little dog barked excitedly, running through the legs of the mules, dodging angry nips from their teeth. In the midst of the preparations for the caravan the merchant's neighbors drank his health and wished him well on his long journey, for it would take many months along the trade routes of Central Asia to China and Arabia.

On his travels he often met people who would ask to accompany him, for his caravan was well protected against attacks by brigands. The merchant had heard many stories from travelers he met on the way, stories of distant lands and strange customs—some spoke of the mighty empire of Rome. Artists showed the merchant ways of writing, painting, and sculpting, unknown to his own people, and philosophers told him of the many ways in which men sought to know the meaning of life. So the merchant's caravan carried much more than wool, cotton, silks, jades, and brocades from country to country—it carried ideas.

One of the merchant's neighbors filled a goblet with wine for him, and asked, since he had no family, who would look after his fine house and warehouse while he was away? The merchant indicated a middle-aged man who was checking the bales of wool. "Jigme will care for my household," he said.

At first the merchant's friends laughed, thinking he was joking; then, realizing that he was serious, they could not believe it. "But Jigme is only a herdsman," one exclaimed. "It is unwise to trust a poor man with wealth," another insisted.

The merchant shook his head. "Jigme is my friend," he said, "he is wise and has a kind heart." But the neighbors still thought the merchant was being very foolish. After all, they muttered among themselves, Jigme was not one of them, he was of inferior rank; some were jealous of Jigme and the trust the merchant placed in him. After arguing unsuccessfully with the merchant one of the men said, "The wise man they call the Buddha is preaching nearby. Will you let us ask for his advice? Remember, your warehouses have our goods in store as well as yours!"

Reluctantly, the merchant agreed. He went with his companions and found the Buddha seated in a palm grove preaching to his followers. Welcoming the merchant and his companions, the Buddha asked them to sit with him while he listened to their story. When the Buddha heard how unwise the merchant's neighbors thought he was, he said he would tell them a story of ancient times, when King Brahmadatta was the king of Benares.

"The king's palace," the Buddha began, "was in a beautiful park, where the king spent many happy hours gardening, and he liked especially to tend his blossom tree. It was the jewel of the park, and he used to look after it very carefully, but neither the king, nor those he took to see the blossom tree, noticed the little clump of kusha grass growing at the roots of the tree trunk. But the spirit of the blossom tree knew all about the kusha grass and its spirit, for the two had been friends for longer than time.

"The blossom tree was mighty and strong, with thick roots that went deep, deep into the earth, reaching into the dark places of demons and monsters. Its trunk was strong, straight, and very high, so that people said its great canopy of branches and foliage reached the heavens.

"No one knew how old the blossom tree was, but it was ancient before Benares had become a great city, indeed, before Benares was even built, and no one knew how long ago that was! And so it was said that the blossom tree was as old as the world itself.

"Everyone saw the blossom tree differently. Some saw it as a mighty and mysterious tree, others as a magic tree, and some, like the king, enjoyed listening to the wind rustling its leaves, which sounded like heavenly music.

"When he was in its shadow, the king was aware of the life of the blossom tree, and it reminded him that everything was like the tree, which grew in the spring and summer, thrusting out leaf-covered branches and new roots, and shriveling in the autumn and winter, leafless, seemingly barren, yet its life went on, and the next year it would burst forth anew. So it told the story of life and death, and life reborn.

"Legend told that the blossom tree, for some who could see, blossomed with the fruit of the secret of life. And sometimes the king had glimpsed for a few seconds among its leaves the most beautiful of blossoming flowers!

"One day, when the king was having tea with the queen in his palace, he was surprised to see something floating in his cup. He looked up at the roof of the room and frowned; small

9

flakes of plaster were falling from the ceiling. He saw that the main wooden pillar which supported the ceiling had cracked and was moving!

"The queen cried out in fear and tried to pull her husband from the room, for she thought that the whole ceiling was going to collapse. But the king asked his wife to leave while he stayed and inspected the damage. He saw that the pillar would have to be replaced as it was beyond repair, and it had to be done very quickly or it would very soon split from top to bottom! He ordered his servants to search the palace grounds for a suitable tree from which the new pillar could be made.

"All that day the servants searched the park, and very carefully measured trees to find a suitable one for the new pillar. After inspecting all the trees in the park, the king's servants realized that there was only one tree that could be used. Sadly, they returned to the palace, and told the king that his beloved blossom tree was the only one fine enough, and strong enough, to replace the old pillar.

"The king was shocked. 'There must be another,' he insisted. 'Maybe one not as strong as the blossom tree, but strong enough to replace the old pillar?' 'Your Majesty,' the servants said sorrowfully, 'in stature and strength, the blossom tree is the only one suitable to make a new pillar.'

"The king was very unhappy, and undecided as to what he should do. If the old pillar split, his whole palace would fall, and his family and many others would be without a home. But there was no other tree in his park as beautiful as the blossom tree. With the queen and their servants, the king went to see the blossom tree.

"Although it was early evening, and the sun still shone, the evening star was so bright that they could see it quite clearly as they walked through the park. The king inspected the blossom tree, and other trees, and even he could see that in comparison it was indeed the best from which to make the pillar. 'Perhaps,' he thought, 'I am being very selfish in trying to keep this beautiful tree which I love, when it could save the home of many. After all,' he thought very sadly, 'it is only a tree, even if it is a special one.'

"So, the king gave the order to his servants, and they prepared sacrifices of penance to the blossom tree's spirit. It was night when the king and queen burned incense and offered sweet tasting delicacies at the foot of the tree. The queen was weeping loudly, as the smoke from the incense fires rose into the velvety blackness. The blossom tree's spirit did not know what to do to save its home, and the gentle breeze quickly carried news of the plight of the blossom tree spirit to all the other tree spirits.

"They gathered around the blossom tree spirit, trying to comfort her and to think of some way of saving her home. Everyone made suggestions, but none was really likely to save the blossom tree. All night long, after the king had left, the tree spirits argued as to what should be done to save the blossom tree, until the poor blossom tree spirit was crying in despair. Then she heard the kusha grass spirit say, in a soft voice, 'Do not worry, my friend, for I have an idea which will save your home.'

"At daybreak, the king's woodmen walked through the park carrying two great axes. They were not singing as they usually did, and the woodsmen noticed that the birds were not singing either. The whole park seemed to be waiting in silence, expectantly.

"The sun remained hidden behind the clouds, shedding only a grey light, and there was no pleasant breeze as they began to inspect the blossom tree to find the best place to start chopping. They were surprised to see that the bark of the tree looked quite different from the day before. Carefully, the head woodsman went round the tree, studying more closely. When he touched the bark it felt soft. 'This tree has gone rotten here,' he said to his companions. He tested another part of the tree, and that too had gone soft! They peered up at the branches of the blossom tree. All its leaves hung limply, as if they were sick and wilting. 'We cannot use this tree to make the pillar,' they said. 'The wood is too soft . . . ' 'I don't understand,' one of

The queen was weeping loudly, as the smoke from the incense fires rose into the velvety blackness.

the woodsmen said blankly. 'It looked so healthy last night, it was the finest tree in the park.' 'I do not think,' the woodsman said thoughtfully, 'that we were meant to cut the blossom tree down.'

"As they walked through the park to tell the king that they had no choice, they would have to make the pillar from one of the other trees, though not such a fine one, the sun shone through the clouds, and the birds began singing, and the little creatures of the park bustled about their business.

"All were happy that the blossom tree was safe, and happiest of all was the blossom tree spirit. All the tree spirits of the park watched the kusha grass spirit with delighted laughter, for before the woodsmen came it had changed into a large chameleon. It had given the secret of how chameleons could change their color to the blossom tree so it was able to change the color of its bark to look rotten when the woodsmen came.

"'But how,' the tree spirits wanted to know, 'were you able to make your trunk seem soft when the woodsman touched you?' The blossom tree laughed, as the

12

kusha grass spirit, in chameleon form, moved over the tree trunk, quicker than the eye could see. Thus, the woodsman thought that the soft body of the chameleon was the bark of the tree.

"The blossom tree spirit sang the praises of the kusha grass spirit: 'Spirits of the trees, for all our mighty power, we knew not what to do, while the humble kusha grass spirit had wit to save my home for me. Truly, we should choose our friends without considering whether they are our superiors, equals, or inferiors, making no distinction. Whether they be tree, bird, or grass, each according to his strength, can help a friend in his hour of need.'

"And so she instructed all the tree spirits, and the assembled devas, saying 'Wherefore such as would escape from an evil plight must not merely consider whether a man is equal or superior, but must make friends of the wise, whatsoever their station in life.' "

As he finished his story, the Buddha smiled at the merchant, who was laughing, for his neighbors, who had thought him so foolish, had received their answer.

The Buddha ended by saying, "In an earlier life, Ananda, my chief disciple, was then the tree spirit, and I, the spirit of the kusha grass."

NOTE: This selection and the one following are two stories of the Buddha's previous lives, from the group best known under the Pali name of Jataka, "birth stories."

SUPPARAKA

ONCE, IN THE GREAT SEAPORT of Bhurukaccha some merchants were making their ship ready for a long voyage. At the same time a famous wise man was visiting the port. Although he was blind, he was by far the most renowned wise man in the whole of the kingdom, known for his great insight and compassion. When the merchants learned that such a great person was in their midst, they immediately sent for him and implored him to join them on their voyage.

"It will indeed be auspicious," said one of the merchants. "He has served the king," said another, "and predicted many things; we must ask him to be our captain!" So eventually the wise man agreed to go with the merchants on their voyage, and the merchants named him Supparaka, meaning captain.

When the stars were visible in the crisp autumn sky and the winds were favorable, they set sail, bound for lands unknown, in search of treasure with which to trade when they returned to Bhurukaccha. For one week they sailed without mishap, and then an unseasonable wind blew up. It tossed the ship to and fro unmercifully on the mighty ocean for many days, until finally they came to rest in a strange sea. The merchants were worried, for they had never been to such a strange place. Fish with bodies like humans and snouts as sharp as razors plunged in and out of the sea. They asked Supparaka,

Men with razor nosings
Plunging in and out,
What sea is this?

Supparaka replied,

Merchants come from Bhurukaccha
Seeking riches to purvey,
This is Waves-of-Razors Ocean
Where the ship has gone astray.

What the merchants did not know was that the ocean was full of diamonds. Supparaka, in his great wisdom, knew this. He also knew that if he told the merchants there would be fighting among them, for greed did strange things to even the most peaceful of people. So, pretending to cast for fish, Supparaka caught instead hordes of diamonds and concealed them on the ship.

They sailed on, driven by strong winds until they came to a sea that was blazing like a fire, like the sun at midday. The merchants took fright and asked Supparaka,

This sea appears like fire,
It is like the sun,
What sea is this?

Supparaka replied,

Merchants come from Bhurukaccha
Seeking riches to purvey,
This is Waves-of-Fire Ocean
Where the ship has gone astray.

In this sea was an abundance of gold, and Supparaka once again took this and concealed it together with the diamonds deep in the ship's hold.

The merchants by this time were getting very worried indeed. For many weeks they had been sailing on seas quite

15

unknown to them and they feared for their lives. They had not sighted land since they had departed from Bhurukaccha, but they seemed to be driven on in directions strange and wild. Navigation was impossible; it was as if some unseen force was guiding them. They decided to return to port, but after they had sailed for several days they found themselves in yet another unknown sea. This sea was gleaming like milk and curds. They consulted Supparaka,

> This sea appears like curds,
> It seems like milk,
> What sea is this?

Supparaka answered them,

> Merchants come from Bhurukaccha
> Seeking riches to purvey,
> This is Waves-of-Milkcurd Ocean
> Where the ship has gone astray.

In this sea there was much silver, which Supparaka hauled aboard and hid from the merchants.

They passed through two other seas, where Supparaka gathered emeralds and precious beryl stones, which he concealed along with the rest of his horde of diamonds, gold, and silver. Peacefully, the ship sailed on for many weeks, but the merchants were baffled by the fact that they had not sighted land for so long although their navigation should have brought them into familiar waters. They were still wandering in seas that they had never before encountered.

Suddenly, and terrifyingly, they came upon a vast ocean, where the waves rose like mountains, and the water swirled furiously, sucking downwards so that it formed a large whirlpool. The swirling of the water, the crashing of the huge waves, and the dreadful roar of the mighty pit as it sucked downwards and downwards made it impossible for the merchants to speak to one another without shouting. They called to Supparaka, in voices raised to hysterical screams,

16

Listen to this terrifying, horrifying inhuman sea,
A sea like a pit and a mountain slope,
What sea is this?

Supparaka replied,

Merchants come from Bhurukaccha
Seeking riches to purvey,
This is Roaring-Whirlpool Ocean
Where the ship has gone astray

Then he continued,

If a ship reaches this sea
No return is possible.

There were seven hundred men on board the ship, and when they heard Supparaka's words they all began to panic. Their wailing and screaming rose above the sound of the dreadful sea, in which they would surely lose their lives; they would be sucked into the huge pit of water and swirled downwards to oblivion.

When Supparaka heard their panic he felt a great surge of compassion for them. He directed the merchants to bring him fresh garments, some scented water and a bowl of food. They did as he requested. Supparaka knew that throughout his life he had tried to do good, never intentionally hurting any living being, and that if anyone could save the ship it would be him.

After he had washed himself in the scented water, Supparaka put on his fresh clothes, ate his bowl of food, then made his way to the bow of the ship. When he had seated himself comfortably, Supparaka made the following asseveration of truth:

As long as I can remember, ever since I've grown up,
I am not aware of having intentionally hurt even one
    living creature.
By this truth, may the ship return to safety.

For four months the ship had been wandering, but now it made straight for port, then traveled eleven hundred cubits over dry land until it finally came to rest at the door of a sailor's house.

Supparaka portioned out the gold, silver, and precious stones among the merchants, giving each an equal share. Then he addressed them, saying,

> With so many treasures you will have enough,
> Never go to sea again.

When he had given them his advice he vanished to a city of the devas.

> In a former life, the Buddha was the
> wise man Supparaka and the merchants
> were his assembly.

TIBET'S FIRST KING

A T THE TIME WHEN the Tibetans were ruled by
twelve petty chieftains, there was much discontent
and fighting as they had no overall leader and were a
country divided. It was during this period that the king of Vatsa
in India had a son. The son was no normal child, for he was
born with turquoise eyebrows, overhanging eyelids, and his
fingers were connected by webs. The king was most distressed
and all the court was frightened by this strange child. The king
wanted to be rid of the boy, so he ordered him to be placed in a
lead box and thrown into the river Ganges. When this task was
completed the king and queen, together with the inhabitants of
the palace, breathed a sigh of reief that they were now rid of the
embarrassing freak of nature.

The boy, however, did not die, for he was found by a
peasant, who on opening the box and finding the strange child
inside was filled with much love for him, and took him home to
live as one of his family. So the boy spent a happy childhood,
loved and cared for by the peasant and his wife.

When he was reaching adulthood the peasant thought that
it was time the boy knew about his strange beginnings, and so he
related the story of how he was found in a lead box by the river
Ganges. So that the boy would not feel that he had been
abandoned the peasant tried to convince him that he was a very
special person, in truth a "mighty one" of high birth. The boy,
however, was saddened when he heard the peasant's story, for

19

he had always believed that he was part of the peasant's family and looked upon the man as his father. In his grief the boy fled to the Himalayas and crossed to the border of Tibet, wanting to spend his days alone in the shelter of the mountains.

There he came across some Tibetan priests of the ancient order, who upon seeing this strange young man declared him a god, for when they asked him who he was the boy answered that he was a "mighty one," and when asked from whence he had come the boy pointed to India across the mountains, but the priests thought that he was pointing to the heavens.

Because of the language barrier they gave up efforts to communicate and the boy was placed on a wooden chair which was set on the shoulders of four men. The priests declared, "We shall make him our lord," and so he was known as "the neck chair mighty one" and was the first king of all Tibet.

PADMASAMBHAVA AND
THE FELICITY SCARF

THERE IS A STORY TOLD of Padmasambhava, the famous Indian teacher, who more than any other was responsible for bringing Buddhism to Tibet over twelve hundred years ago.

It is said that the Tibetan king, who was not a Buddhist, deeply resented the reverence and honor the people of Tibet were showing to the great Indian teacher Padmasambhava. Indeed, it seemed to him that the people revered Padmasambhava more than they did their own king! So the king decided to make sure that when the great teacher visited him, all the country's leaders would see this man, whom they honored so much, pay homage to their king.

On the day of Padmasambhava's visit all the courtiers were assembled to watch him pay his respects to their king, who waited to acknowledge the great teacher. The haughty king could hardly conceal his delight when Padmasambhava raised his arms as if to prostrate himself before the royal throne, but flames darted from Padmasambhava's hands and ignited the king's clothes, which were ablaze in seconds. As courtiers beat out the flames, the king, stifled by the smoke rising through the folds of his ceremonial scarf, tore it from his shoulders. Realizing the great teacher's power, he threw himself at Padmasambhava's feet in submission and offered the scarf to him as a token of humility. Padmasambhava accepted the scarf, then returned it to the king, draping it

Flames darted from Padmasambhava's hands and ignited the king's clothes, which were ablaze in seconds.

around his neck as a blessing and signifying the victory of spiritual over temporal power.

And so it is said in Tibet, a land of few flowers, that Padmasambhava established the giving of katas, or felicity scarves, as a gesture of respect.

NOTE: The kata, or felicity scarf, is a long piece of white cloth which may vary in quality from fine silk woven with religious designs to plain gauze stiffened with rice powder. The literal meaning of kata is "cloth that binds," thus it symbolizes a bond or connection between the giver and the recipient. For Tibetan lay people the exchange of katas is a form of greeting, but with rather more significance than shaking hands has in the West. Introductions and meetings are much more important in a country seven times the size of France but with a far smaller population—a traveler can go for weeks without seeing another person or habitation and must rely on the hospitality and acceptance of villagers and townspeople, former strangers, for the replenishment of supplies, for housing, and for a place in which to conduct his business. The exchange of katas under these circumstances expresses a mutual desire to establish harmonious relationships and engages the participants in certain responsibilities toward each other.

Gift-giving is a basic custom among Tibetans and katas are symbolic gifts of purity and respect. Other gifts are wrapped in katas for formal presentation. When a person presents a kata to a lama, it may be returned to the donor as a form of blessing and sign of special connection between the two. Thus the kata also symbolizes blessing and represents the activity of bodhisattvas who continuously give their compassion and concern for mankind. The giving of gifts comes to have a religious significance which transforms material concerns into spiritual activity, indeed another name for katas is "divine fabric."

Just as the Romans, Greeks, and Egyptians decorated their ancient temples with garlands of flowers, the Tibetans drape their connection with the spiritual realm and open them to receive blessings. Pilgrims drape katas on shrines, around images, over sacred thankas, and throughout temples. Freshly starched katas lie beside those presented years before and which have become as fragile as spider's webs with the passage of time.

What you write with ink in small
black letters
Can all be lost through the work
of a single
drop
of
water.
But what is written
in your mind
is there
for
eternity.

—Tsangyang Gyatso

How Asanga Came to See the Future Buddha

ASANGA, THE LEARNED SAGE, his heart set on realizing the inner wisdom, meditated in retreat for many years. The object of his meditation was Champa (Maitreya), the buddha of the future who resides in the Tushita heaven awaiting his descent to earth. Asanga was patient in his endeavors, but even he, after many years of earnest meditation, was beginning to be frustrated with his attempts to attain the wisdom he desired.

One day, while taking a walk outside of his cave, Asanga noticed some birds landing on nearby overhanging rock. Where the birds' wings brushed the rock as they landed, Asanga noticed a deep crevice had been worn in the rock. Asanga reflected on the countless number of years it must have taken for the soft brushing of birds' wings to make such a deep indentation.

On returning to his cave, Asanga, his senses sharpened by deep meditation, heard the soft drip of water over stone. On closer examination he found a small rivulet of water running down the rock face; over the years the gentle dripping of the water had cut a deep pathway into the rock.

"If birds' wings and water can cut into rock," Asanga thought, "then so can I, through meditation, cut through the thought layers of mind and so attain wisdom." So, Asanga continued to meditate, but still without result. It seemed the more earnestly he sought wisdom and the more passionately he tried to invoke Champa, the more impossible it became. Asanga left his cave to search for food, and came upon a man rubbing a stout iron bar with a piece of cotton. Asanga inquired of the man what he was doing, and the man replied that he was making a needle. Asanga was amazed that the man should consider it possible to make a needle by rubbing soft cotton over a thick iron bar, and when he said as much, the man replied, "If a man is really determined to do something, he will not meet with failure, even if the task is seemingly impossible."

Asanga found renewed strength, believing his task no harder than that of the man making the needle, and returned to his cave inspired to continue with his meditation. After he had been meditating for twelve years, still without result, Asanga finally decided to leave his retreat and give up his meditation on Champa, for Champa would not appear to him, even after so many years of trying.

On leaving his retreat Asanga came upon a dog mad with pain from a wound in its side which was infested with worms. Asanga felt great compassion for the dog and wished to relieve its suffering, but knew that if he removed the worms from the dog's side, then they would surely die for lack of food. Asanga decided to remove the worms, and place them on his own flesh so that they could continue to live. Just as Asanga reached out to remove the worms, he held back. "If I remove them with my fingers," he thought, "then I may crush them." So, closing his eyes, Asanga leaned forward to lick the worms from the wound in the dog's side. Just as his tongue touched the dog, it disappeared, and in its place, bathed in a pool of brilliant light, appeared Champa, the future buddha.

Overcome with emotion, Asanga spoke to Champa: "For so many years and in so many ways I have tried to see you. Why now—now that my thirst is gone, do you appear before me?"

Champa replied: "It is only now, through your great act of compassion, that your mind is pure and therefore able to see me. In truth I have been here all the time."

Then Champa instructed Asanga to carry him on his back into the city so that other people might see him. This Asanga did, but the people, their minds clouded by impure thoughts, could not see Champa, and they thought Asanga was mad when he cried that he had Champa on his back. One old woman who looked and saw a puppy on Asanga's back was immediately endowed with riches. A poor porter caught a glimpse of Champa's toes, and from that moment onwards attained power and tranquility of mind.

Champa then took Asanga to the Tushita heaven, and there he was able to receive the teaching and gain the insight that had eluded him for so many years.

NOTE: Asanga was born in Gandhara and lived during the fourth century. Tibetans consider him one of the "Six Jewels of India," along with his brother Vasubandhu, Nagarjuna, Aryadeva, Dignaga, and Dharmakirti, all of whom made important contributions to Mahayana Buddhism. Asanga and Vasubandhu are said to have founded the Yogachara school of Mahayana Buddhism. Asanga sought to realize the inner wisdom of the sutras (Buddha's sermons) by meditating on Champa (Maitreya), the future Buddha, in order to gain insight and knowledge of the teachings.

The story is typical of Tibetan Buddhist stories in its emphasis on the balance between wisdom and compassion in their dynamic aspects, that is wisdom as insight as well as knowledge, and compassion as a positive force that enables one to work for the welfare of all beings rather than a sentimental approach to the ills and sufferings of others. Wisdom without compassion is ineffective because one cannot make use of wisdom without the motivation of compassion; conversely, compassion without the insight of true wisdom becomes shortsighted and often ego-oriented. In Tibetan iconography wisdom and compassion are symbolized by the bell and dorje (vajra) often held in the hands of a deity.

GESAR OF LING

For more than a thousand years the people of Tibet have sung of the warrior-king, Gesar of Ling. With the passing of the centuries the epic has grown so that a bard singing the story today will take up to six hours a day for several weeks to complete the entire epic. There are many episodes in the story and it is not unusual for different bards to develop their own sequences of episodes. The story that follows tells of Gesar's birth and of how he became king of Ling. The essential story line remains the same in all the tellings of the epic, but their settings and expression vary. Our story is drawn from a series of frescos in Samdu monastery in Kham, the eastern province of Tibet, where Kusho Ralla was a monk. Although there are a few manuscript copies of the epic it is essentially part of Tibet's oral tradition, memorized and handed down generation after generation.

Gesar, the warrior-king of Ling, is to Tibet, what St. George is to England, the national hero, the conqueror of evil. But perhaps Gesar is a little more, for he is the just king, the protector of the poor, the defender of Buddha's teaching. There seems little doubt that Gesar is a historical figure, and indeed until the recent changes brought about in Tibet by the Chinese occupation, there was a king of Ling who was recognized as his descendant. But the warrior-king has also grown in stature with the passing of the centuries: the Manchu emperors, for example, worshiped him as the god of war, and many see in Gesar echoes of Caesar—news of the Roman conquerer traveled to Tibet with merchants on the silk route.

27

The national dress of Tibet's three provinces; Kham (the East), U-Tsang (central Tibet) and Amdo (North East Tibet). The fold over the chest forms a pocket (ambac).

To the Tibetans Gesar still lives, and the additions to the story are the natural consequences of his revealing more of his life. Although the story is meant to be entertaining, it is also regarded as having a deeper significance, and anyone telling the epic would at the very least believe himself inspired by Gesar; bards go into trances when relating his life and are believed to be in direct communication with the warrior-king. To ordinary people Gesar is such a living reality that when they travel, they will sing whatever snatches they know of the story as invocations for his protection on their journey. Gesar's world of fantasy and magic is no less real to the Tibetans than the world in which we live, for they regard both as "images in a dream." They say the fantastic events in the epic result from Gesar's harmony with and knowledge of the forces of the universe, so that he could influence and use them, in much the same way Western scientists now employ nuclear energy and laser light.

The epic of Gesar has become the national story of Tibet, but to the people of the Land of Snow it is not just past history: it contains many prophecies of Gesar's return to Tibet, so the epic is also a guarantee to Tibetans that once again their land will know the rule of a just king in a free realm.

IT IS SAID THAT many centuries ago the kingdom of Ling, famous for its piety and the wisdom of its sages, was to suffer a time of great unhappiness. Darkness, the shadow of revenge, was to fall over the people, and the light of the dharma would be extinguished. Such a night, never to be relieved by the dawn, was to come about because of a woman who thought her unhappy life was the result of the Buddha's curse. Vengeance and hatred filled her heart, so that her dying wish was to be reborn with her three sons as rulers in Buddhist kingdoms and so be able to take vengeance on the dharma, the Buddha's teaching.

Padmasambhava, the "Lotus Born," also known as Guru Rinpoche, or the "Precious Master," realized the intensity of the demonic power that would be unleashed by the dying woman's wish, and sought to save the three kingdoms in East Tibet where she and her three sons would be reborn. At Guru Rinpoche's request the bodhisattva Thubpa Gawa agreed to incarnate among the men of the kingdom of Ling, and to fight the dark powers which would rule the kingdom and its principalities. Guru Rinpoche chose as the mother of the incarnate bodhisattva a young naga, one of the serpent spirits of the water. Nagas can easily transform themselves, and so the spirit had no difficulty in assuming the form of a young and very beautiful girl, who came to be known as Gongmo.

The girl walked many miles through the kingdom of Ling accompanied by a mare, a cow, a ewe, a she-goat, and a bitch. As Gongmo approached the capital of Ling she saw that there were crowds of people around the great gate to the city. They were obviously waiting for someone. Gongmo's arrival in the city caused much laughter, for everyone knew that Tondon, the

29

steward of the kingdom, had seen many omens indicating the arrival of a great being who would change the history of Ling. For this the townspeople had been waiting at the city gate, but to their delight, only a beggar girl and her few animals came to Ling that day! Even so, Tondon did not let his hurt pride sway his belief in the omens. He decided to learn more about the beggar girl, and so arranged for her to be taken into the service of his sister, the queen of Ling.

It was not long before Gongmo became a familiar figure in the community, and frequently the subject of the local men's talk and attentions, for she had an unusual beauty. Her perfectly formed body and the compelling luster of her eyes were combined with a grace and charm of manner that was even more attractive because of its innocence. Her qualities would have marked her out anywhere, but they were certainly unusual in a herdswoman, and it was not long before the queen, enjoying Gongmo's company, arranged for her to work much of the time in the household. Gongmo was now often with the queen, who foolishly did not foresee that her husband, King Sining, also would awaken to Gongmo's attractions. After a time they had fallen deeply in love, so that the king was determined to take Gongmo as his second wife.

The queen was furious, both at the king's evident love for Gongmo and at the popularity among the people of the king's proposal. She did everything in her power to dissuade the king and refused to agree to his taking Gongmo as his second wife, but the queen knew that this would not deter him, and that there was only one way to make certain that she alone was the king's wife and the queen of Ling. The queen arranged for Gongmo to take the yak herd to new pastures. Gongmo's suspicions were aroused since she could not see any reason for the change, and she remembered hearing vague stories about the area to which she was being sent.

At the false dawn Gongmo stirred the yaks into activity with calls and pebbles from her sling on their insensitive rumps. Anxiously the queen watched from an upper window as Gongmo urged on the great ambling yaks, bellowing at being disturbed. To reassure herself Gongmo spun a prayer wheel as she walked, murmuring its mantra OM MANI PADME HUM, the physical activity helping to focus and concentrate her thoughts.

The way to the pastureland passed through a narrow ravine; Gongmo felt increasingly nervous at the reactions of the yaks, who bellowed furiously and stubbornly refused all coaxing and threats to get them to continue. Very slowly she managed to move them on, but when they were far into the ravine she realized that there was no sound, except the growing protests of the yaks. No bird calls, no rustle of breezes in the stunted grass, no movement or sound from any insect. Nothing. Complete silence. Gongmo began to feel very frightened, too frightened even to turn the prayer wheel as she began to think that this valley must be the one in the stories, the valley of the silent ones.

It was said that strange and evil beings were trapped in the valley because it was the only place without sound—there they found relief and sanctuary from the agony they suffered at even the slightest noise. As Gongmo remembered the stories she stopped walking and looked about her with dread, even afraid to breathe, her rapid heartbeat filling her ears so that it sounded like thunder in the valley. The yaks snorted and stamped the ground as they clustered together; Gongmo could feel their apprehension. She remembered hearing that anyone who ventured into the valley of the silent ones and made the slightest sound caused the silent ones so much pain that, in their desperate anger, they slew the intruder without mercy.

Gongmo turned suddenly, feeling herself being watched, but there was no sign of anyone, or anything, in the bleak treeless valley with its contorted rocks and boulders. Yet her feeling grew into an appalling certainty as she became aware of not just the presence of someone, or something, intently watching her, but of numerous presences circling closer, unseen, silent, stifling. She gave a frightened, unbelieving cry and tried to run from the invisible ring, but it made no difference. In desperation she called on Guru Rinpoche, as she felt herself being invaded by the invisible forces and in her mind's eye glimpsed their awful forms.

As she cast about for some way to escape the entities that were suffocating her mind, her very life force, the ravine was transfused with light, and became transparent as she sank in despair to the ground. Her vision was clouded by the light as she weakly murmured appeals to Guru Rinpoche. The light grew brighter as Gongmo's weakening eyes searched, hungered for release. Everything was fading from sight—the sky, the ravine, the earth—in the irridescent golden light which became a thick mist that enveloped her. Now Gongmo was sure she was dead and in the bardo realm.

Dimly, Gongmo realized she was free of the oppressive forces that had stifled her, but it took a few moments for her mind to adjust. Her fear only slowly dispelled in the soothing light. The mist thinned to reveal a beautiful rainbow arching up into the heavens. Around the rainbow the golden light grew more intense, thickened and solidified, taking shape so that within moments the figure of the great diety Kenzo appeared. His body was like a living image of gold, and as he slowly descended the rainbow Gongmo saw that he held a holy water vase, with a peacock feather sprinkler fanned from its top. In a voice like the thunder of the heavens, Kenzo said to her, "Guru Rinpoche heard your call and so I have come." He bent towards her, holding out the vase. "The water within this vase has held the reflection of bodhisattva Thubpa Gawa who is to incarnate among the men of Ling. Drink this water and in due course you shall bear the incarnation of Thubpa Gawa, he who will be a dharma-warrior, the king of Ling."

The queen was horrified when she came across Gongmo churning cream in the kitchen, and realized that the girl had escaped from the valley of the silent ones. The two women looked at one another and the queen had no doubt that Gongmo understood the terrible trap into which she had been sent, but Gongmo said nothing, not even to the king.

The months passed and Gongmo, feeling no sign of pregnancy, began to wonder if indeed she would be giving birth to the incarnation of Thubpa Gawa. But one day when she was sitting on the flat roof of the house the remarkable golden light that had heralded the approach of Kenzo appeared again, and again a beautiful rainbow formed, stretching across the sky and leading straight to the house. From all parts of town people came running to the king's house to see the signs in the sky that could only mean the coming of a great being. Within the house there was a considerable amount of confusion, no one knew why the king's house should be so honored. In the uproar Gongmo slipped down the stairs to her room and carefully closed the door behind her. The crowds outside were both frightened and fascinated at dancing lights that suddenly appeared around the house. Few people noticed that Gongmo's cow, ewe, she-goat, and bitch all gave birth at this time, as did her mare to a superb foal with a silvery coat, a "blue" horse, a "horse of the gods."

Gongmo waited, nervous and uncertain. She had a very strong feeling that the rainbow and the dancing lights heralded her child's entry into the world. But, she thought, looking dubiously at her belly, such an evident lack of any sign of pregnancy did make her wonder if she was not deceiving herself. Just occasionally during the months she had vaguely felt an awareness of another life within her, but it was so fleeting, she could not be sure.

"Oh mother!" A voice, to Gongmo's amazement, came from her stomach. "Now is the time of my birth. Be not afraid, turn your mind to Guru Rinpoche." This was indeed no ordinary child, she thought, settling herself on the divan, and feeling rather shaken that her as yet unborn child could already talk! The golden light gradually filled the room, she felt it penetrating every fiber of her body. As she meditated she unconsciously lifted her hands to her head to receive an emerging sphere of glowing light.

"We must prepare for the great Lama." The king was standing on the flat roof of his house with his queen. Both looked with awe at the light flooding from the rainbow, and could feel its energy. The queen murmured, "Perhaps we are to be honored for what is . . . and not for what will be . . . " The king looked at his wife sharply. "Explain! What have you heard?" The queen smiled at him and rested her hand soothingly on his arm. "Nothing. I have heard nothing, husband. But I just say what could be . . . " As she turned to go, the king gestured for her to stay with him. He knew that she was not telling him all of her suspicions. "I am going to have the house searched," the queen explained. "There has to be a reason for . . . for . . ." she gestured to the rainbow, "this." The king looked down at the crowd around the house; many of them were chanting prayers.

Gongmo held the globe to her breast and felt the tiny heartbeat within. Smiling, she felt the globe move and stretch in her hands, and the baby struggling to release himself. Her baby. Gongmo was filled with a sense of wonder and love, as the tiny babe struggled into the world, breaking free from his eggshell of light. Gongmo was far more conscious of the miracle of the baby himself, than the manner of his birth. After cleaning him, she nursed him, singing a lullaby as she cradled him in her arms.

The door of Gongmo's room flew open and the queen just caught a glimpse of the child enveloped in golden light as the girl hid the baby in the folds of her dress. Within seconds the celestial light evaporated. Gongmo looked at the queen with a mixture of fear for her child and an aggressive determination to protect him. The queen was not really surprised; somehow, she had known. Slowly she entered the room as Gongmo watched her with dread, realizing there is no worse enemy than a former friend and even greater enmity when the field of battle is a husband.

"My Lady, please . . . "

Gongmo's restraining hand was like a feather as the queen pulled back the folds of the girl's dress. Both women gasped in amazement. In a matter of moments the infant had grown to the size of a year-old child. He fixed the queen with dark compelling eyes; the queen backed slowly away, longing to flee the intense gaze.

In the courtyard of the house the queen looked drawn and anxious as she spoke to the servant who was soothing his restive horse.

"You have mentioned the message?"

"Yes Highness."

"Then take it swiftly to my brother, the steward Tondon." She turned away, muttering "May he have the answer to this curse upon our lives!" Angrily she spun the prayer wheels set in niches in the wall.

Tondon, the steward of Ling, was discussing his revenues with his chamberlain when he received the queen's messenger and news of Gongmo's strange confinement. Agitatedly Tondon ran his hand over his close-cropped hair. His chamberlain could not help thinking that his master looked just like a worried rabbit with his buck teeth emphasized by his thick moustache curling around his mouth and out across his cheeks.

"It is happening! It is happening!" Tondon wailed. "As prophesied, it is happening."

At first neither Tondon's wife nor his chamberlain could understand him. Then he reminded them of the ancient prophesy.

"It tells," Tondon said, "of a young girl who will arrive in Ling with five animals, just like Gongmo, and who will give birth to a magic child, who will become a great and victorious king of Ling."

Both the Chamberlain and Tondon's wife could see that while the fulfillment of such a prophecy might be pleasing for Ling, it would be a considerable disadvantage to Tondon, who would certainly lose much of his power and revenues.

Angrily Tondon ordered his horse saddled, then rode alone through the streets of Ling, causing many who saw him to reach for their beads and whisper a prayer. For the noble steward of Ling to ride unaccompanied did not augur well, especially when his face betrayed his terrible anger. He knew that his only chance was to act decisively and swiftly, without mercy to his enemy.

"Where is the child?"

Fear flooded through Gongmo as she heard the threatening voice in the corridor outside her room; desperately she looked for some means of hiding her child, but there was no place. As she thought of how they might escape, the door crashed open. Tondon stood in the doorway, his great body wrapped in a satin chuba, heaving with exertion. Behind him, his sister, the queen, stood looking nervous.

Tondon, his fat hands outstretched, bore down on Gongmo as she backed away.

"I have seen the strange signs, signs that show you have given birth to a demon," Tondon shouted.

"It is not true!" Gongmo was weeping, and cried out as she felt the unyielding wall behind her, leaving her helpless before Tondon. He tore the child from her. She flung herself at him, attacking him with all the force in her body, and the crazed desperation of a mother defending her offspring. The queen screamed at the terrific blow Tondon gave Gongmo, it sent her sprawling into a corner, and she had to look away when he swung the baby high in the air and repeatedly smashed the child's body against the wall. Eventually the queen could stand it no longer. "Stop!" she begged. "Tondon. Please! He must be dead by now!" Tondon dropped the limp body onto the floor. His face was streaming with sweat; vigorously he splashed his head with water from the leather pail.

Gongmo moaned with pain and grief.

Suddenly the queen grabbed her brother's arm. Tondon turned.

"Ama-la? Ama-la?" The child was standing, grown to the size of a two-year-old, gently stroking his mother's head and apparently completely unharmed by Tondon's brutal battering.

36

"Now!" Tondon shouted at Gongmo, who drifted in and out of consciousness, "Say that this child is not a demon?" He snatched a rope from a hook in the wall and grabbed the baby, deftly binding his hands and feet. The child caught Tondon's eye for a moment and the steward found himself meeting the gaze of someone far older than a child of a year, let alone a few hours. The child's eyes frightened Tondon with their challenging mocking look. As he picked up the bound child, the little boy shouted to his mother, "Do not fear, Ama-la. Have faith." But even as he spoke Gongmo hurled herself at Tondon, scratching, kicking, and biting for her child. Tondon, frightened by the ferocity of the attack, yelled for his sister to help him and struggled to keep his hold on the infant. The queen held Gongmo, enabling Tondon, his buck teeth working up and down as he puffed with exertion, to tear himself free and run with the child to the courtyard. He could not, dared not, look again at the baby's eyes, but he could feel them on him.

Tondon ran, harder than he had ever run before, and hurled the infant into the household rubbish pit in the corner of the courtyard. "Devil child," Tondon shouted, as though to convince himself as much as anyone else, and to drown out Gongmo's moaning, despairing cries. Using all the energy he had, Tondon manhandled an enormous millstone from where it had been leaning against the wall of the house to the edge of the pit. Tondon thought the exertion would kill him as he toppled the stone so it fell and completely sealed the top of the rubbish pit. Tondon staggered and clutched his chest, he thought his heart was going to collapse.

A few hours later, after he had rested, Tondon was mounting his horse in the courtyard and saw Gongmo lying on the millstone, distracted with grief, as she tried in vain to pull the stone from the pit. Tondon rode his horse out of the courtyard, keeping his eyes ahead, toward the gate.

The days passed without any word of the child. The queen sent her brother a message reassuring the steward that he had finally succeeded in destroying the infant. But Tondon's mind would not rest. It was haunted by thoughts of the child, by a dreadful fear that he still lived. No matter how often he tried to dismiss the doubts he always ended by asking himself how any child could have survived the battering he had given it. What child could almost walk and certainly talk only hours after birth? Would such a being really lie entombed, defeated beneath a millstone? He had to be sure. Trusting no one but his wife, Tondon sent her to the king's house to personally check the pit.

Hearing of her arrival, the queen went down to the courtyard to greet her sister-in-law. The two women found it difficult to make themselves heard above the laughter of the servants who filled the yard as they watched a performance by a group of strolling players. "See!" The queen pointed at the great millstone lying across the mouth of the rubbish pit. "It is undisturbed." The two women smiled at one another in relief, then stiffened, fear chilling them at the bubbling childish laughter behind them. They turned to find a small boy, about four years old, looking up at them both intently. Surely, Tondon's wife thought, this cannot be the child, it is ridiculous to even think such a thing. . . . The child laughed, gently, but knowingly, mockingly, then darted away among the crowd. Now the steward's wife knew. The child lived! The queen had known the moment she looked again into the child's eyes, not the eyes of a child but of generations.

As Tondon's wife hurried back to tell her husband the terrible news, Gongmo walked across the courtyard and looked for her son. The little boy saw her and held high a stiff piece of tattered brocade. Smiling at his pleasure in this makeshift flag, she picked up the child, praising the gods who had restored her child to her, alive and well, only hours after his entombment.

Tondon paced up and down the room.

"This is surely the future king of Ling, of whom the prophecies speak! Unless we find some way to be rid of this demon we are all doomed!"

He glowered at his council. The men sat on cushioned divans, looking acutely embarrassed at their helplessness and very conscious of the truth of his words. Only Tondon's plump wife appeared unmoved by her husband's rage as she sat on a seat beside, but slightly lower than, her husband's.

"We need a powerful magician to help us," she said. "Someone used to controlling demons."

Tondon stopped pacing. "The hermit Ratna!" he exclaimed, shouting with joy.

On a rocky promontory, bare of vegetation, hermit Ratna had his hermitage, where he spent long annual periods in retreat. For the rest of the year he lived in a fine monastery, built among the woods at the foot of the mountain.

Tondon struggled up the stony track, cursing as he repeatedly cut and bruised himself on the rocks. He thought bitterly how typical it was of the hermit to have such an inaccessible place as a hermitage. By man's curious reasoning, Tondon had observed, which interpreted situations according to its own wishes and prejudices, the pilgrim's anticipation of meeting a holy man at the end of the path would only be increased by the inaccessibility of the hermitage. When Tondon at last reached the hermitage, he found Ratna sitting inside waiting for him.

"Welcome, I have tea ready to refresh you." The hermit poured them both some boiling hot liquid from a clay teapot. Tondon paused a moment to catch his breath before entering beneath the crude wooden awning above the mouth of the cave, which served to prevent the rain from driving into the hermitage. The hermitage was sparsely furnished, but the view was superb; one could see the whole valley and Tondon could not help but feel a sense of wonderment at the beauty of the woodland spread out below. Entering the cave, Tondon bowed before the great Ratna and draped a long felicity scarf across the low-carved table, set before the cross-legged hermit. Carefully, he placed a beautifully wrought silver butter lamp on the scarf, and as a container should not be offered empty, he placed a huge rough-cut turquoise in the bowl of the lamp. Ratna's eyes flickered on the lamp for a moment, then he draped a scarf around Tondon's neck in greeting and blessing. Tondon muttered his thanks, sucking in his breath as a sign of respect, and took the seat in front of Ratna, who offered him some fruit. Tondon was disarmed that the hermit had prepared for his visit. In all the years he had known Ratna he had never shown the fat man any indication of having telepathic powers, though he was reputed to be a powerful, if greedy, magician. The hermit waited for Tondon to begin the conversation, but he found it difficult to do so before Ratna's intense eyes, enlarged and emphasized by his bony and emaciated face.

Indeed, Tondon felt so embarrassed at the thought of the hermit's apparent telepathic powers that he could not gather his thoughts enough to explain his problem. His buck teeth rose and fell over his lower lip, as he struggled to articulate his thoughts.

"You fear," the hermit said abruptly, breaking the silence, and sounding slightly impatient, "that this boy, whose mother came from nowhere, is the future king of Ling spoken of in the prophecies."

The spell was broken and Tondon replied passionately. "It is true! It is true! I am as nothing before this child." Tondon paused to make sure the significance of his words had been fully understood by the hermit.

"Rinpoche," Tondon flattered with the title of a great lama, "with my own hands I have done everything to kill the child, only hours after his birth. No human child could have survived. Yet he did not have a mark on him, he laughed at me! What am I to do? I am doomed if this child lives to become king!"

The hermit Ratna watched Tondon and smiled slightly, his long fingers automatically fingering the amber beads of his rosary.

"What size is this demon child?" he asked thoughtfully.

"In hours he grew from being a babe in arms to being a young child that can walk, and talk, but he is still quite small."

"Good," Ratna said briskly. "Now do not worry, I will deal with the child demon." It was clear to Tondon that Ratna had brought the interview to a close.

Gongmo's baby, whom she had named Gesar, although only three weeks old looked at least four years and when he spoke it was with a maturity of mind and such wisdom that his mother felt he was as old as the gods. Yet the child was a strange mixture, for he still had all the mischievous playfulness of a little child. After talking with him, Gongmo accepted his adult mind without question, but then would look on amazed as her young son ran out of the house to play and fight happily and uninhibitedly with the other children. He did perfectly normal things, but there was always something about the way he did them that was unusual. Gongmo reflected on the time Gesar made a bow. He went to extraordinary lengths to find a special type of tree from which to fashion the bow, and to her surprise, insisted on using strands of her hair to make the bow string.

Gongmo watched her son as he sat putting the finishing touches to the bow, his usually mobile face set in concentration. She had to admit that Gesar was not a very handsome child, certainly he did not have the sort of face one would associate with a child of the gods. In fact his broad, frank smile, laughing eyes, and snub nose made it far more believable that he was a child of the nomadic bandits. But when he talked with Gangmo about his mission, he became serious, his whole personality seemed to change and he showed a compelling and definite charisma.

Terrible screeching filled the air. Gongmo ran to the window, "Gesar, what is it?"

She looked up and saw three enormous birds circling over the house, like vultures over carrion. "What are they, Gesar? Never have I seen such birds!" As Gongmo went outside for a better view, Gesar held his mother's arm.

"No Ama-la, do not go outside."

"Why? Tell me! What is going to happen? What are these birds, Gesar?"

The screeching was directly overhead. Gongmo slammed the window shutters and bolted them. Gesar did not reply. The little boy, no more than eighteen inches high, with bare buttocks beneath his tiny sheepskin chuba, was concentrating totally on putting the final touches to his bow. His nimble fingers worked on silently, as though racing against time.

"Holy gods, they're going to attack us!" The cry of the birds had an urgent threatening quality. "What shall we do?" Gongmo backed away from the windows and grabbed hold of Gesar as the room darkened and the shutters shook violently, wings beating against them. Gongmo instinctively held the child close, both to protect him and to seek reassurance. She looked down at Gesar, her "magic" child, small round face, dark, wise eyes; but still he was a child. Suddenly he slipped from her hold and stood alone in the middle of the room as the shutters of one of the windows splintered and for a few seconds, framed in the window, Gongmo saw an enormous bird filling the room with an eerie metallic rattle from its shimmering black feathers, its metal beak flashing with reflected light, the edge as sharp as a well-honed blade. As the bird launched itself at Gesar, the child, who already had an arrow on the bow, loosed it, a fragile wand only a few inches long. It pierced the bird's feathers. The creature screamed with pain, arched its body, then fell so close to Gesar that the point of its beak touched Gesar's leg and drew blood.

Gongmo was terrified at the viciousness of the creature and ran to the window. Already the other two birds were preparing to swoop through the window.

"No Gesar!" Gongmo ran over to him as he struggled to lift the bar from the door. He looked up at his mother.

"Do not fear Ama-la. Let me go to meet them. It is better."

Gongmo hesitated, then reluctantly unbarred the door for her son. Swiftly the birds came out of the sky, close together. As they dived toward Gesar, Gongmo saw townspeople crouching on roofs and in doorways, terrified by the malevolent looking creatures. Quicker than the eye could follow, Gesar fired two arrows. Each found its mark and the two birds fell from the sky.

Gongmo ran to her son and soon they were the center of an enthusiastic crowd with Gesar being carried around the town as a hero. Already, most of the people of Ling had heard of the strange little boy, rumored to be the natural son of the king.

Tondon was furious when he heard the news. His rage alternated with desperation at what seemed the inevitable outcome of his struggle with the boy. He was even more out of humor when he had climbed again to Ratna's hermitage. The hermit was sitting outside the cave and clearly expecting Tondon. The steward thrust a scarf at the hermit, who was slightly disconcerted by his client's changed attitude.

"Well? Your news?"

"You do not know," Tondon sounded faintly sarcastic, "that your metal birds have been destroyed by this devil child?"

Hermit Ratna was shaken. Tondon continued, "I am lost. There is no one else who can do anything. You were my last chance."

The hermit irritably spun a prayer wheel on the table to relieve his feelings.

"Do not be troubled," he said, trying to sound persuasively confident. "It was a trial. I do not expect you to understand the subtleties of my actions," he said airily. Tondon knew enough about the hermit and his ways to see that he was trying to cover his error. Tondon wiped the sweat from his forehead with his sleeve and said, "Rinpoche, remember this. If this devil child becomes king, you, all of us, will be in danger."

"I am a hermit," Ratna replied, "what need I fear?"

Tondon laughed. "There will not be a hermitage, no matter how dark and how hidden that will not fall to his searching gaze."

Ratna's lips tightened. He gave an empty bitter smile.

"Tondon, order the boy to come and see me tomorrow."

Tondon's plump face was still beaded with sweat from the climb. He wiped his brow again on his sleeve. "Rinpoche, what do I do if the child does not come? How do I make him come?"

"He will come," Ratna said quietly and lowered his eyes in meditation.

Tondon was left alone with his apprehension and the ringing of a tiny bell that marked the turning of the prayer wheel.

Gongmo was working the paddle in the wooden tea churn, mixing the butter and salt with the freshly brewed tea, when the messenger found her in the kitchen.

"What does a messenger from the steward Tondon want with me?" she asked apprehensively.

"You have a child."

"Yes." She reached behind her to clasp Gesar's hand. The little boy was hidden behind her skirts.

"He is to attend the hermit Ratna tomorrow."

The others in the kitchen, who had gradually slowed their work as they listened to the conversation burst into laughter. A heavily built woman who was the housekeeper seized hold of Gesar and held him high for everyone to see.

"This babe is meant to climb a mountain? I think the noble steward asks the impossible!"

"Perhaps his mother is meant to take him," someone said.

"Remember who killed the metal birds," a voice shouted.

"He is indeed a remarkable child." The housekeeper kissed Gesar loudly.

The tiny child with the cascading laughter turned to the messenger. "Tell your master, the noble steward Tondon, that I shall go to see the hermit Ratna tomorrow."

Gongmo looked at her son, silenty reproachful. He chuckled, saying, "Have faith in me, Ama-la."

Gongmo smiled, but her large eyes filled with tears.

Despite Gesar's reassuring words Gongmo's heart ached as she watched her son set off on the long journey to the hermitage. She had provided him with barley meal and dried cheese cubes in a bag that he carried over his shoulder.

From the windows of the king's house the servants and Gongmo watched Gesar's slow progress, for he was still a very little boy indeed, and Gongmo was convinced that he would not reach the hermitage before sunset, but he had refused to let her go with him. As he walked through the fields people stopped their work to ask him where he was going, and when he told them, many joined him, singing and laughing, carrying Gesar on their shoulders to the hermit Ratna. As they climbed the steep path the sharp breeze caught the clouds of felicity scarves draped around Gesar's shoulders, gathering up the lightest and lifting them like feathers floating in the wind over the valley.

It was a long and arduous climb. As they neared the hermitage Gesar could hear the dry, rapid beat of the damaru drum used to invoke the deities. He asked to be lowered to the ground so that he could approach the hermitage alone. As Gesar turned the corner he saw that the hermitage was empty and his eyes were drawn upwards. Ratna, his deep-throated chant accompanying the drum, was sitting, dressed in the bro-cade robes of his personal deity, levitating some twelve feet from the ground. The pilgrims with Gesar were awestruck by this display of spiritual power. Some of them saw more than others. Terrified, they turned to force their way through the crowd and back down the narrow track.

Like Gesar they had seen the enormous shadowy figure towering behind the hermit, with its dozens of arms fanning out from each side of its body, each arm moving, supple and snake-like, and grasping a different weapon of destruction. Its bull-like head moved impatiently; its three eyes searched as though it hungered for destruction; its whole being throbbed with power, only held in check by Ratna. For many hours he had meditated on this being, until this yidam, his personal deity, had appeared before him, charged not only with its own power but also the concentrated mental power of the hermit.

Gesar approached closer to the hermit. The deity held no fear for him; he knew it was only the fierce aspect of a power that could also be compassionate and gentle, and that power was always terrifying if one did not understand it. None of the pilgrims followed Gesar, for even if they could not see the deity, they could sense its presence.

Ratna had fixed the little child, not two feet high, with a terrible stare. The stocky Gesar looked back unwaveringly at the hermit and slowly wiped his nose on his grubby arm. The hermit was disconcerted and his concentration was momentar-ily lost; he dropped fully three feet in the air. Ratna intensified

45

the rapid beating of the damaru drum, twisting it back and forth in his hand so that the leather thongs hanging from it beat a rapid tattoo on the drum faces. The hermit paused in his chanting and said severely to Gesar, "Which demon gave you birth?"

Gesar laughed loudly and looked up at the hermit with a mocking air, his head on one side. "Surely such a great hermit and magician as you knows who my parents are?" The child did a handstand, and standing on his head, gazed in silence for some time at the hermit, who was, to say the least, unsettled by his total lack of success in intimidating the child.

"You know of my mother Gongmo, surely?"

Ratna did not deign to reply.

"She is one of the fairest of the nagas, chosen by Guru Rinpoche himself to be my mother, just as the bodhisattva Thubpa Gawa was chosen to be my father."

Ratna began to sink slowly to earth, like a pricked balloon. He knew now that this was to be the greatest test in his life.

Gesar continued to stand on his head and watch Ratna who, still chanting and beating the drum, unfolded his legs as he neared the ground and entered his hermitage, still in the demonic shadow of his yidam. Ratna sat on the low divan in front of the shrine.

Gesar, who had carefully turned himself around so he could face the hermit, although still upside down, said, "Tell me Ratna, which is the real hermit Ratna? The one I see now or," he dropped to his feet and stood up, "the one I see now?"

The hermit was not inclined to reply or engage in metaphysical debate, but feeling he had to retain some control of the situation abruptly ceased drumming and said, "Neither has any objective reality. My form is passing. It changes every moment. But the potential for enlightenment within my mind shines as a lamp in the darkness forever."

Gesar smiled, "Some will seize hold of the lamp to lighten their whole mind, while others will use its light to work in the shadows."

Ratna picked up one of the carefully made tormas, pyramid-like cakes formed of colored dough, and infused it

46

with the destructive power of his yidam. He hurled the torma at
Gesar, who deftly caught it and then reverently set it down on
the ground, picking up a small piece that had broken off. He
looked at it and then at the hermit.

Ratna sat rigid, unmoving, frozen with fear.

"Why are you a hermit?" Gesar asked, and the magician
felt dread at the calm note in the boy's voice.

"That I might help people, little demon," Ratna shouted
defiantly, helplessly.

"Then surely such a strict hermit as you shall be of the very
greatest help to people." Gesar laughed and raised his arm to
throw the piece of torma.

Ratna stood up and extended his arm in mute appeal, but
Gesar had already thrown the piece of torma. It hit the rock
with a grinding roar and turned into an enormous boulder that
slid down and fell across the entrance of the cave, entombing
the hermit.

News of the battle of magic between Gesar and the hermit
quickly spread through the town, and it was not long before
Tondon heard of Ratna's defeat. In despair, and fearful of
Gesar's growing popularity among the people, he banished
Gesar and his mother to a distant and uninhabited valley.
Tondon ordered the leading lamas and citizens of the town to
escort the child and Gongmo into exile, enforcing his order by
leaving them in no doubt as to what would happen to their
hostage if they did not carry out his order. Tondon did not
really think this banishment of Gesar would free him of the
threat the child posed, but at least he thought it might postpone
it.

When they reached the solitudes and the valley of banishment, the little group of townspeople sadly left Gesar and
Gongmo, but not before helping them to find a cave for shelter
and leaving them with plenty of provisions. They urged
Gongmo to travel on and to find refuge in another kingdom,
but they knew that few left the solitudes, for many demons

dwelt among its bleak and cavernous rocks, and danced upon stony wastes.

Gongmo held the little boy's hand as they silently surveyed the vast plain, the surrounding mountains so distant they looked like soft blue mounds, a mirage on the horizon. In the far distance a herd of wild asses appeared from the haze and galloped across the plain, so small in the distance that Gesar was reminded of flies he had seen running across the rice paper window in their room in the house at Ling.

Days, months and years passed. Three years after their banishment, Gongmo and Gesar were still traveling the solitudes, for though Gongmo still talked of finding a place where they might settle and perhaps farm, they had set out many times only to find that they had returned to the heart of the solitudes, so that Gongmo knew in her heart that Gesar did not intend them to leave, not until he could return to Ling. In three years he had grown into a handsome, if unkempt, youth, who daily became more attuned to their nomadic existence. By the time their provisions had run out, he knew exactly where to find wild berries, what to hunt and where—his senses had become as sharp as any animal's. A change in the wind, a bird call—Gesar understood their every significance.

But Gesar was not always successful at providing them with food, and one day while they were sitting disconsolately drinking tea, thinking of their hunger, they became aware of a rainbow that stretched across the plain and formed a beautiful tent where it touched the earth. Realizing that they were to be honored by celestial visitors, Gongmo and Gesar searched among their belongings for scarves to present. Guru Rinpoche emerged from the irridescent tent. He received their scarves of homage, and then reminded Gesar of his mission, that the child was fathered by a bodhisattva to fight against the dark forces which were bringing unhappiness to the land. Guru Rinpoche declared Gesar to be king of Ling, urged him to use all his abilities and wisdom to take possession of his throne, and assured him of the support of the gods. He told him about eight treasures he had to find in order to overcome his enemies when he would be king of Ling. Then Guru Rinpoche withdrew into the rainbow tent, which slowly ascended into the sky and was gently enfolded by the clouds.

So many months had passed without Tondon hearing anything of Gesar or his mother, surely, he told himself, he could feel confident now that he had finally outwitted the devil child. But like a recurring twinge of toothache the doubt would return, like a ghost of the dead, like a fearful herald of the prophecy's fulfillment. In an attempt to gain some mental rest, some assurance, Tondon decided to spend a period in retreat and meditate on Tamdin, a diety who was his yidam, his guardian and guide. Surely, he thought, Tamdin would show him the truth and release him from this tormenting uncertainty.

For many days Tondon meditated alone. A servant left his meals in an outer room, so that no one, and nothing, disturbed him. He meditated before a large and beautiful shrine. The outer wall of the shrine room gave onto a red-painted carved wooden balcony. One day after Tondon had been meditating all morning and was beginning to feel definite pangs of hunger, a large blackbird silently alighted on the balcony rail. For a few moments it quickly looked around the room. Tondon was startled out of his meditation by the rapid beat of wings as the blackbird flew into the room and settled on part of the carved canopy of the shrine. For a moment Tondon looked at the bird in disbelief, confused as to whether it was part of his meditation or an actual blackbird that had flown in through the window. In either case he thought it could only be of significance, for blackbirds were most auspicious. After carefully grooming its flight feathers, running them through its beak, the blackbird turned its attention to Tondon.

"I am a messenger of the gods, noble steward Tondon." The blackbird spoke in a soft lilting voice. Tondon could not believe he was to be so fortunate. It had been years since he had received such direct guidance from the gods, why, long before he had become immersed in his responsibilities as steward of

Ling. The blackbird continued, "King Sining will not be return-ing from his pilgrimage to the holy places in India."

At first Tondon did not understand what the blackbird was saying.

"You must announce the king's death to the people of Ling, and then you . . . "

Tondon had already begun to protest; how would people believe him if he said that he had received this message from a bird! But the blackbird was continuing its message for Tondon and was clearly not going to be interrupted.

"You must prepare for the enthronement of a successor. Inform the people that the throne will be occupied by the most worthy, by the chosen of the gods, for the skill of the candidates will decide who is to be king. A race will be held in which all the men of Ling can participate. It will last two days and will prove who is the most worthy to sit on the throne, to be king of Ling."

Tondon was not very happy about this arrangement, and he was just going to try and explain to this blackbird the problems involved when the blackbird said reassuringly, "Do not worry, Tondon. Choose the best horse you can find, and there will be no doubt about the outcome." The blackbird paused, cocked its head to one side, and looked at Tondon intently as though to give him time to realize the significance of what he was saying. After a few moments he said quietly, "I am the voice of the precious master."

At the mention of Guru Rinpoche, Tondon was convinced. This was indeed, he thought, a message from the gods.

The blackbird had apparently completed its message. It become absorbed in grooming its feathers while Tondon thought about what it had said to him. Watching the bird at its toilet made Tondon think how very normal, even handsome a blackbird it was, indeed he really began to feel it looked too normal, and he started to wonder if he had imagined it all. He had to be sure.

"Is it true?" he said softly, feeling acutely embarrassed, and fearing both that he might upset the bird or be proved deluded.

The bird ignored him and went on grooming, vigorously scratching its beak with one foot.

"Did I imagine it? Please say something!"

Suddenly the bird stopped scratching, and holding its foot in mid-air said testily, "I have told you."

Tondon, with some difficulty, as his legs were stiff after sitting in meditation for so long, prostrated himself, from sheer emotional gratitude, before the blackbird, and held aloft a scarf. The bird flew down from the shrine, plucked the scarf from Tondon's hand and left some droppings on his head. These Tondon reverently removed with another scarf, while the blackbird dropped his scarf over the shrine and flew away through the window. Tondon ran to the balcony in time to see the bird swiftly flying towards the woods on the mountainside.

Tondon threw open the doors of the shrine room and, bursting with his news, pounded through the corridors of the house shouting for his wife and chamberlain, so the whole household heard him. His wife and the chamberlain came running up to him, greatly agitated, feeling certain that something dreadful must have happened.

"Summon the council. I have vital news for them!" Tondon said breathlessly.

"When do you want them to meet?" The chamberlain asked.

"Now!" Tondon shouted impatiently. "Tell them to come here immediately, this will be the most important meeting of their lives. It affects the whole kingdom." Tondon was holding on to the wall to steady himself he was so out of breath. The servants who had overheard Tondon quickly relayed his words to other members of the staff and soon the whole house and neighborhood were full of rumors.

"Sound the great drum," Tondon said to the chamberlain. "I wish all the people of Ling to hear news of great importance."

"What is it, Kusho?" His wife put her arm around him to support him, for his face was scarlet with the exertion and excitement. Tondon dismissed the chamberlain and walked slowly back to the shrine room with his wife, telling her of the extraordinary message he had received from the gods. Her silent and unimpressed reaction angered him.

"Do you not remember how I used to receive such messages," he said peevishly, as though to remind her that this was not the only time that the gods had honored him.

"I remember indeed, Kusho," his wife said gently "but it is just this message that I am not convinced about."

"*This* message! Why, this is the most important one of my life!"

She stroked his head and attempted to soothe him. "That is why we must be very careful. If it was a trick it would be disastrous."

"How can it be a trick?" he asked scathingly.

His wife did not answer him, but poured some chang to cool her husband. She knew from the concern that filled his eyes that he was beginning to see her point. But the bird's message was too much of a lifeline, of an escape from all that he feared. He had to believe.

"Get out!" he shouted and a bowl of fruit narrowly missed her head. Then like an enraged yak he chased his wife from the room, while she yelled back warnings of woe and misfortune.

Neither Tondon nor his wife had noticed the blackbird, the "messenger of the gods" perched on a branch of a tree overhanging the balcony, chuckling quietly to itself. It was a laugh Gongmo would certainly have recognized.

Tondon was not alone in remembering Gesar. Already he was a folk hero, and many talked of his coming back to Ling some day, for was he not a "child of the gods?" Many wanted Gesar to ride in the race for the throne of Ling. Some of these supporters were eating at the house of Tsering, the richest man in Ling, and arguing about how they might find Gesar and Gongmo to tell the boy of the race. It was known that there were many traps and dangers for the traveler in the solitudes, and who could tell where Gesar and his mother had gone by now in those vast plains; it could be weeks, even months before they were found.

"I will find him for you." Everyone stopped talking and looked in astonishment at Dolma, the pretty, young daughter of Tsering.

"Dolma! Dolma!" Her father laughed. "Why will you be able to succeed when none of us, who have years of experience traveling the mountains and valleys, can be sure of finding Gesar?"

"Because, Pa-La, I know in my heart that Gesar is destined for greatness. Because I know that my destiny is to help him."

The guests were silent and then murmured to one another. Dolma was a very unusual girl. At her birth the lamas had said that she was an especially blessed child. Although Tsering was very reluctant, eventually he agreed with his guests, and Dolma's sincerity convinced him, that the gods had chosen her to be their messenger.

The following day at dawn Dolma, dressed in a peasant's chuba and with saddle bags bursting with provisions, set out on the route described by her father, who was one of the group that had taken Gongmo and Gesar to the solitudes.

Many lonely days passed; only once did Dolma come to a village, a tiny hamlet of six houses where she stayed the night. Occasionally she saw the splash of a monastery's white walls set high among the rocks of a mountain, the temple roofs reflecting the sun in their gilded tiles. But gradually all sign of human activity disappeared as she went on across a vast grassy plain, and into the solitudes, beneath the glacier-tipped mountain peaks. Dolma sang,

> When you have arrived beyond the pass,
> The great high mountain will cover you with its shadow,
> Though I call you I will hear no word.
> When you go down into the valley,
> Where lies the most precious jeweled lake,
> You will go down into its waters,
> But I who have exhausted my good karma
> Will be left by the side of the waters . . . .

Dolma's sad lover's refrain reflected her thoughts as she rode the empty, stony plain, the bells on her horse's harness no longer sounding joyous but melancholy as they emphasized the silence, the emptiness of the land. Dolma fought off despair, determined to find Gesar, certain that with the blessing of Guru Rinpoche she would succeed.

Three days later Dolma was getting worried about finding Gesar in time for the race, and she began to wonder if perhaps he and Gongmo had managed after all to travel to another land, another life. But still Dolma felt, despite everything, that Gesar's life lay with the future of Ling. She was falling asleep with exhaustion as her horse took her over a rise—stretching into the distance was yet another vast plain—but here she caught sight of an outcrop of rocks with a cave, its entrance sheltered by a tattered awning. Excitement and anticipation flooded through Dolma as she urged her horse ahead. This had to be where Gesar and Gongmo lived, she thought. A few yards ahead she noticed a marmot suddenly appear from its hole, sit bolt upright on its haunches, and gaze intently at her, nose twitching vigorously as it anxiously sniffed the air at the approach of the horse. Something flashed past the head of Dolma's horse and the marmot was knocked off its feet and lay dead. Turning in the saddle, Dolma saw a young man striding toward her. He was about sixteen with wild, unkempt black hair, dressed in a sheepskin chuba, and holding a sling. He looked just like any number of nomad boys she had seen, but there was a quality about his smile, and as he came closer she saw something in his eyes.

"Gesar!"

The youth laughed with delight on hearing his name called, and helping her to dismount, teased Dolma on how beautiful she had become since he had last seen her in Ling. As they walked toward the cave, Gesar deluged her with questions, desperately wanting to make up for being so long without any news.

As they neared the cave, Gesar, still walking, stooped, picked up a smooth round stone and slipped it into his sling. He stopped, whirled the sling around his head, his eyes trained on another distant marmot that had incautiously appeared from its hole. Instinctively Dolma put a restraining hand on his arm, but Gesar launched the stone killing the animal instantly. Gesar sounded faintly mocking as he said "Do not worry Dolma. These animals are not what you think! Gesar walked over to the body of the marmot and held it up for her to see. They are creatures who can change from this harmless appearance to demons who torment the spirits of the dead." At first Dolma thought he was teasing her, then realized that he was perfectly serious.

When they reached the cave, Dolma hesitated to go in, it looked so filthy, and used the opportunity of unharnessing her horse to put off the moment, but even when she had unsaddled and tethered her horse she made no move to enter the cave.

"Dolma, I know this is not what you are used to, but you will never receive warmer hospitality. Come and meet my mother Gongmo. You will make her very happy." Dolma smiled, but her step toward the cave was obviously reluctant; it was so very filthy. She screamed as the body of one of the marmots Gesar had killed hit her on the head. Angrily she turned on Gesar. He was laughing and this so enraged her that she ran to hit him, but as she raised her small fists to strike she saw that her arms were covered with loose clumps of black hair, She clasped her head. To her horror she realized her hair was falling out with even the slightest movement of her head.

"My hair! Gesar! My hair! What has happened!?" Dolma wept while her hair gently continued to fall, sticking to her tear-streaked cheeks. Smiling, Gesar leaned forward to touch her head. Instinctively Dolma drew back, fearing the slightest touch would cause even more of her hair to fall, but Gesar ran his hand through her hair, as she cried out in despair, but no more hair came away in his hand. She touched her head. Her hair felt as thick and luxuriant as before. Laughing with joy, Dolma tentatively pulled at a lock. It held. She tugged. Not a hair left her head. Dolma looked at Gesar and wept with joy. Gently he untied her plait and drew her waist-length hair over her shoulder, running his hand though it so that she could see that the light shimmering through her hair formed the mantra OM MANI PADME HUM. Dolma looked at Gesar for a few moments, her heart filling with love, then, laughing, she aimed a blow at him in mock anger at his teasing.

"Even the humblest cave can hold riches." He smiled; Dolma understood and followed him inside. There was Gongmo in a tattered dress, looking very dirty and unkempt. She greeted Dolma warmly and made a place for her to sit. Dolma gave them gifts of food from the people of Ling, and while they enjoyed the fine tea, which Gongmo and Gesar savored after drinking nettle tea for so long, Dolma told them about her mission and the race. Gongmo was concerned that if they returned to Ling, Tondon might try to kill Gesar again.

"But no one will recognize him." Dolma knew this was not true, but she hoped it would reassure Gongmo.

"My destiny is Ling's destiny," Gesar said quietly.

A few hours later Gesar and Dolma sat on a rock in the sun and talked as they watched a small herd of musk deer. Gesar took a thin rope from his shoulder, saying he had to kill one of the deer, and asked Dolma to help him. She was not at all happy about the suggestion, for she did not believe in the taking of life. But, laughing, she asked, "Are you going to say it's another demon?" "Yes," Gesar said, and Dolma really did not know whether or not to believe him. But she helped him. Stealthily Gesar worked himself into the browsing herd of deer without causing them to panic and run. Slowly he took the rope from his shoulder, and swiftly, silently, whirled the lasso; the deer became apprehensive, then they all started running. The noose snaked out over the head of one of the stampeding deer. The animal reared up in terror, then wildly hurled itself in all directions, struggling to free itself of the noose. Gesar played it like a fish, slowly bringing the rope in. The small animal with the delicate body, weaving and dancing at the end of the rope, was using every ounce of its energy to pull itself free. It danced around Gesar, then suddenly darted away, so that before Gesar realized it the rope was twisted around his neck and then tightened. Gesar struggled to free himself, but now the deer was the captor, the hunter, rather than the victim. Dolma ran to help but she found that no sooner had the deer slackened the rope for a second than it would tighten again; it was like fighting against some demonic intelligence, she was sure the deer knew exactly what it was doing. Gesar threw himself to the ground in an attempt to free himself from the strangling rope. He was gasping for breath, choking as Dolma tried to free him. Desperately she turned on the deer and tried to grab it, then without thinking as she heard Gesar groaning, she picked up a stone and as the deer darted past her, without thinking she brought it down as hard as she could on the animal's head, killing it instantly. She ran to Gesar and helped him tear the rope from his throat. He gulped at the air, then staggered to his feet and walked slowly across to the deer. Dolma watched him. "It's dead," she said finally, sadly.

Gesar jokingly chided her for killing a defenseless creature.

"But it was a demon."

"I may know that, but I wonder if others will believe it?"

Dolma was upset that her family might hear of her having killed the animal, for they were very religious. She was angered by Gesar's attitude, especially since she had just saved his life, but he made light of the episode and teased her even more, promising to keep her secret if he could have her whip.

"I'll give you my whip!" Dolma shouted. She ran to her saddle and harness, siezed the whip from a rock and then chased furiously after Gesar, trying to beat him with the whip, until they both fell exhausted and laughing to the ground. Thus Gesar acquired the first of the treasures described by Guru Rinpoche.

Gesar and Dolma realized that if they were going to return to Ling in time for the race, they would have to ride hard, so it was agreed that Gongmo would follow on behind at an easier pace. As they galloped across the plain, Dolma felt very unhappy that Gesar seemed to think so little of her, that he could tease her so unmercifully. Gesar was thinking of Tondon, of his subtleties and tricks. There were, after all, many greater magicians in Tibet than the hermit Ratna whom he had defeated three years previously. It occurred to him as certainly not beyond the realm of possibility that Dolma was a phantom, conjured up to trick him. He prayed it was not so, for he knew now how he felt about her, but for this very reason he had to know, or the question would always be there. He spurred on his horse, whispering in its ear.

"Gesar! Wait! I cannot keep up with you," Dolma shouted. Suddenly Gesar's horse lunged forward, its body like a clenched fist of taut muscles. Then to her horror Dolma saw the horse bolt. She shouted, and Gesar shouted back at her, but she could not catch what he said as he struggled to bring the horse to a halt, pulling its head around to slow it. Dolma spurred her horse on. As Gesar's horse neared the long grass of the river bank, a fore hoof slipped on a marmot burrow, and the horse fell, throwing Gesar violently from the saddle. He disappeared into the long grass. The grass was so tall that for a moment, just after she dismounted, Dolma could not even see Gesar's horse; then it staggered to its feet. She ran over to it and saw that it seemed to have no broken bones. But there was no sign of Gesar.

"Gesar! Gesar? Where are you, Gesar?" She walked slowly through the long grass looking for him, worried that he had been knocked unconscious, yet not able to put the idea out of her mind that all the time he was playing a joke on her.

"Gesar if you do not come out I'll ride on without you!" But her threat brought no response, and as the time passed and she walked on, Dolma grew more apprehensive. Then she saw his hand in the long grass. She recognized his silver saddle ring, and lying near by she noticed the whip she had given him.

"Gesar . . ." As she parted the grass Dolma's mouth opened in a silent scream that took moments to tear itself from her being. It was Gesar's arm, but the grass had parted to show the bloody stump of the shoulder where it had been severed from his body. Feeling she was in some terrible nightmare and unable to understand how it could have happened, Dolma wandered through the grass. She looked down as she accidently kicked something and felt it roll beneath her foot. She was looking into the lifeless eyes of Gesar's severed head. Her tears mingled with his blood as she murmured again and again, unable to believe that he could really be dead, "Gesar, Gesar, do not tease me."

Wracked with grief, Dolma called on Guru Rinpoche for help. Her long black hair fell over her face as she looked down at Gesar's head cradled in her arms, tears nearly blinding her.

"Dolma!" At first Dolma thought it was her mind playing tricks, as she heard the familiar voice. "Dolma."

She opened her eyes. There was no sign of Gesar's head or body. "Dolma!" She turned.

He was sitting, restored and healthy, cross-legged and balanced on the slender curve of a two-foot-long stalk of grass.

"Gesar!" She ran to him. "I thought that you were dead." Dolma was overwhelmed with an emotional flood of anger and relief. She pummeled him in a rage as soothingly Gesar tried to defend himself.

"Why Gesar? Why put me through such pain? Why?"

"I had to know, Dolma." He stood up and held her face in his hands. "Now I know that there is no deception or trick, that your heart is your own, that I do indeed have it, as you have mine."

Gesar and Dolma rode beside the surging river of the Ling valley, its fields of barley ripe for harvesting. Even from a distance they recognized the portly figure of Tondon approaching with a group of riders. Dolma hoped she would not be recognized in her peasant chuba. As the party of riders approached, Gesar realized that Tondon was looking at him and his horse intently, even while he continued speaking with the rider beside him. Dolma glanced nervously at Gesar and lowered her head. They eased their horses to the side of the path so Tondon and his party could pass them without hindrance. As Tondon's party went by, Gesar bowed his head in respect to the steward and drew in his breath. Then, just as he and Dolma were urging their horses onward, Tondon shouted to Gesar. "Nomad boy! I want to speak to you!"

Gesar realized it was fruitless to ride on with Tondon's friends all around them. He turned his horse and, with Dolma following, walked the few yards back to Tondon. Gesar dismounted to approach, hoping his deference would help to prevent the steward from recognizing him.

"Your horse is very fine," Tondon said. He was carefully appraising the horse. It was without doubt the finest he had seen, and he was remembering the words of the prophecy: ride the finest horse in Ling to be sure of winning. This horse must be, he thought, the one he should ride.

Tondon's companions had gathered around Gesar and Dolma, each voicing opinions on the horse. Gesar received congratulations on his mount which inspired considerable admiration in all of them. "Would you consider selling it?" Tondon had little hope that he could persuade Gesar to sell it; as a fine horse was far more valuable than its monetary worth.

If Gesar was unwilling to sell, Tondon thought, he would have to think of some other means of acquiring the horse. Gesar politely discounted the virtues of his horse, explaining that Tondon's horse was better in various points. Tondon held out his hand and Gesar took it. Tondon offered Gesar a substantial amount by the means of a hand grip, the movement hidden by his long sleeve. Gesar declined, and so Tondon increased his bids, until he realized that Gesar was unresponsive from lack of interest in a sale, despite being offered a fortune.

"Kusho," Gesar said, "with respect, I do not wish to sell my horse."

Tondon threw Gesar's hand down angrily. There was a hardness in his voice when he spoke.

"I would like to try your 'humble' beast!" The breath hissed through his back teeth.

Gesar paused for a moment. "You will honor my horse and myself." He wanted to do anything to avoid suspicion.

Tondon's servants dismounted quickly in order to help the steward dismount from his own horse and mount Gesar's.

"Where did you get this horse?" Tondon asked.

"From my uncle. He has fine horses."

"Why will you not sell him, even for a fortune?"

"I cannot, Kusho, he is my mother's."

"But I thought you said that he came from your uncle." Tondon tapped a small jade bottle onto his hand and inhaled some snuff.

"From my uncle's herd."

"Would your mother think of selling him?"

"She knows very little about horses, Kusho."

"Then why does she need a horse like this?" Tondon sounded exasperated.

"One does not only have what one needs in this life," Gesar replied.

"Can you tell her I am interested in buying her horse?"

"I will not be seeing her for some six months."

"You are on pilgrimage?"

"Yes," Gesar replied, "but my mother does not know anything about horses."

"But since she owns it, I would have to buy it from her?" Tondon asked.

"Well," Gesar sounded thoughtful, "she would ask my opinion. I am the only one who really knows about him since I ride him."

"But you said he wasn't your horse."

"He isn't."

Tondon was growing angrier by the minute. "I have already asked if I can buy the horse from you."

"Well," Gesar said "it would depend on my uncle."

"But you said your uncle had given the horse to your mother."

"He has."

"Then explain to me."

"My uncle wants to breed from the horse."

"So I have to ask your mother, who will ask you, who will ask your uncle. But your uncle will have to ask your mother who will ask you?"

61

"Er yes, Kusho," Gesar smiled. Tondon hit the horse with his whip, determined now that he would have it, and mentally cursing Gesar for all eternity. As he rode past, some of his companions pointed at the horse. Tondon reined in, and asked them what they had seen.

"The horse has a double joint."

Tondon did not believe them, and got Gesar onto the horse so that he could watch its movement closely. To his horror he saw that the beautiful beast did indeed have a double joint. It would be hopeless for racing, Tondon thought, and felt even angrier that he had not noticed it earlier and had wasted so much time. His friends were clearly finding the whole thing hilarious. Feeling humiliated and uneasy, he climbed back onto his own horse and urged it into a rapid pace.

Dolma rode beside her father, dressed in her festival clothes and attended by their household, listening to the dull echo of their horses' hooves in the deserted town square as they rode to join the townspeople camped at the picnic ground for the start of the race. Dolma's father looked across the square at the large carved and gilded throne set up on the temple steps, awaiting the winner, and beside it the slightly lower throne for the new queen of Ling—Dolma. *His* daughter, queen of Ling. He glowed with pride when he looked at her. Already she looked the part in a chuba of brocade satin edged with otter fur, her hair in a hundred plaits gathered into a single braid and interwoven with ornaments of turquoise and coral. Looking at the empty thrones Dolma felt both apprehension and excitement. Her father had promised her to the winner of the race. If it was not Gesar she would lose him forever, but if he won she knew she would be his wife and queen.

The rolling turf of the picnic ground on the outskirts of Ling was churned up by the five hundred horsemen, milling and shouting as they attempted to get all their horses lined up beside the shallow stream which was the starting line.

Almost the entire population of Ling had come out to see the race. Many families had set up their picnic tents, which were decorated with brightly colored felt designs, and innumerable fires heated cauldrons of water for the enormous tea pots. The two-day-long race had become a festival for the whole country and everyone was dressed in their finest clothes. When they were not watching the race it would be a time of dancing, singing, feasting, drinking, and gaming. Tondon glanced up at the monks setting up the ancient canon on the monastery ramparts, in preparation for the starting signal. A groom led his horse through the crowd toward the edge of the stream. Many people had been unhappy that Tondon was participating in the race, for some said that such a powerful figure would put everyone else at a disadvantage, but Tondon realized very rapidly that no one was going to allow him to win the race out of awe or respect for his position and rank. Those men who courteously acknowledged him before the race, Tondon was quite aware, would fight him relentlessly during it. The steward smilingly acknowledged the greetings, then his smile froze as he noticed someone on a horse a few yards away. It was the young nomad boy he had seen the day before. Tondon was very puzzled to see that his horse appeared to be perfectly fit with no sign of a double joint. It was as he had originally thought, a superb horse. Even as he realized this, Tondon also recognized the boy's smile and the look in his eyes. Tondon moaned aloud. Gesar had returned!

The cannon on the wall of the monastery was fired in a cloud of billowing smoke before anyone expected it, startling some of the horses so that at least twenty of the riders were thrown at the starting line. The rest of the competitors careered across the stream, and in the jostling mass more riders and horses fell.

The terrain was such that the winner of the race would not necessarily be the fastest runner, but the toughest, the best able to endure the pressure of the race and the harshness of the course. Tondon had made careful preparations: along the route were grooms and servants carefully disguised as farmers, pilgrims, or monks, with refreshment and even fresh horses. Even though the gods had assured him that he would win, he believed it was up to him to make sure he would realize the prophecy!

Gesar had made a very poor start. Hemmed in at the back of the mass of horsemen, he had been brought down within seconds of the start by a falling horse. Some hours later he adjusted the eyeshade of fringed cloth which protected his eyes against snow glare as he plodded toward the mountain pass. The snow was churned up with hoofprints and the footprints of other competitors. A handful of riders were scattered over the mountain, wearily climbing the track toward the pass. Gesar paused to give his horse some tsampa, then chewed a cube of dried cheese.

At noon the sun was harsh. Gesar and his horse walked with dragging feet along the edge of the lake, so vast that he could not see the far shore. He wore his sheepskin chuba with the sleeves tied round his waist, leaving his torso bare to the sun. Gesar looked longingly at the water, so enticingly refreshing, but it was salty and undrinkable. About a hundred yards ahead Gesar saw three other competitors. One, too exhausted to walk, was riding a horse that looked ready to drop. As Gesar walked through some apricot trees he saw a strange figure sitting on a medong—a wall of stones engraved with invocations. Drawing closer Gesar realized that the young man was a hunchback, his body twisted and contorted so that it appeared as if one side of it had been lifted higher than the other before his bones had set, giving him a hump, a limp, and leaving his head on one side. But the young man had a cheerful countenance and greeted Gesar while he filled his hat with water from a large container and gave it to his horse to drink. Gesar looked longingly at the water bottle as he walked up to the young man. The hunchback smiled and offered the bottle to the youth. When Gesar had given his horse a drink from his cupped hands, he took some himself.

Gesar was exhausted and, looking at his horse, knew that they had to rest if they were to have any hope of going on. He sat

on the wall with the young hunchback, and felt utterly drained
of energy.

"What is your name? Mine is Gesar."

"Greetings Gesar. I am Chamba, the riddle maker."

Gesar laughed at the man's title and, nodding his thanks as
the young man handed him the water bottle again, took another
drink. While he drank Gesar took in the young man: he was
dressed very colorfully, with a red chuba, saddle rings on every
finger like a nomadic bandit, and a beautiful bow and quiver of
arrows. The quiver especially caught Gesar's attention. It was
covered in sharkskin and bound in silver.

"Tell me some riddles," Gesar said as he handed the water
bottle back.

The young man laughed. "No, I shall tell you of the
possible that is impossible, or the impossible that is possible."
He laughed again, and Gesar thought that he must not stay too
long or he would lose the ground he had made up.

"How could one louse fill your hand to overflowing?"

"How?" Gesar asked.

"Why, if its muscles are unravelled they will fill both your
hands."

Gesar pulled a wry smile. He saw a rider approaching in the
distance.

"How," the hunchback asked again "can one ant fill a
tsampa bowl?"

"I do not know," Gesar replied.

"The drop of blood from an ant's nose will fill a tsampa
bowl."

The rider was fast coming up to them. Gesar, instead of
feeling refreshed was feeling more and more tired.

"You talk nonsense," he said. He tried to walk away from
the wall, but found he was too weak to do so. As he glanced at
the hunchback the young man smiled back at him, with his
curious laughter. The rider cantered past.

"But you must hear the third impossibility."

"Well," Gesar said, and tried to summon up all his
energies.

"A magpie that gives birth to a baby and gives it milk."

"It is not hard to think of impossibilities, riddle maker."

"But mine are possible, think carefully."

Gesar shook his head in disbelief, he was so tired.

"Tell me three things sharpened by nature?"

"I don't know," Gesar wanted to get on, if only he could get up enough energy. He forced himself off the wall and stood up.

"A tusk, a horn, and a splinter of wood."

Gesar smiled and tightened the girth of his saddle, as the young man limped across to help him. Swiftly he slipped a burr beneath the woven saddle rug. Gesar swung up into the saddle, and was about to bid farewell to the hunckback, when his horse, reacting against the pain of the burr, lashed out with its hindquarters, catching the hunchback in the side and knocking him into the lake.

"Help me," the hunchback yelled. "I cannot swim! Help me!"

Gesar quieted his horse, jumped down from the saddle and saw a thin trickle of blood oozing from beneath the saddle rug. He felt beneath it.

"Shall I help you," Gesar angrily shouted, "as you have helped me?" He held aloft the burr.

"Please," the hunchback was treading water and managed to grab hold of a slippery rock to which he desperately clung. "I had to do it. I am sorry, but the steward Tondon ordered it."

Gesar walked to the edge of the lake, looked calmly at the struggling hunchback, tossed the burr into the water and said "We will strike a bargain. For your fine quiver, I will rescue you."

"Anything," the hunchback gasped. His hands slipped on the rock. "Help me!" He disappeared beneath the water.

Gesar took the rope from his saddle and hurled it out into the water. It was quickly grasped by the hunchback, and Gesar pulled him onto the bank. As he lay wet and frightened on the ground, Gesar took the quiver from him, slung it over his shoulder, and remounting his horse spurred it into a gallop to catch up with his competitors. He had found another of the treasures of Guru Rinpoche.

When dusk fell Gesar rode on through the night, with only the pale ghostly light of the moon. Sometimes when it disappeared for minutes behind clouds, his horse would stumble, its hooves slipping into one of the holes of the tailless-rat warrens. Gesar slackened his pace but still rode on.

It was some hours after midnight when he was riding through a wood that he saw, in the shelter of some rocks, the glimmer of a campfire. Gesar approached cautiously: it was unusual for a fire to burn brightly at this hour, and who could say what evil spirits might be abroad waiting to catch the unwary traveler. As he drew closer Gesar saw the glint of firelight on the long blade of a sword held at the ready.

"Do not fear," he shouted. "I am one of the competitors in the Ling race. Who are you?"

Gesar was by no means certain that the sword was only for defensive purposes! A gravelly woman's voice answered. "Come into the light where I can see you."

Gesar dismounted and, leading his horse, walked up to the lone figure beside the campfire. She was a plump middle-aged woman, her chuba bag was stuffed full, and she carried two sets of saddle bags filled with the equipment and medicines of a doctor. As the doctor sheathed her sword, Gesar had no doubt as to her capability with it. She heated water on the fire for tea, and he unsaddled his horse to give it a rest.

As he talked with the doctor, he was increasingly fascinated by her hat. Like a giant bird's beak, it was made of tightly woven bird's feathers. They appeared to be a form of cloth, so closely did one feather lie against the other. The doctor, Gesar discovered, was on her way to a nomadic encampment for the winter. After they had eaten and talked for a while, Gesar asked for the doctor's opinion, saying that he had felt unwell for some time. The doctor gave him a thorough check, gently feeling the subtle veins of energy in his body, and eventually declaring him to be perfectly healthy. Gesar accepted this doubtfully. A short while later, Gesar said he definitely was not well. Again the doctor wearily went through her tests, and again she reassured him that there was nothing wrong with him.

"But I now that there must be. Why would the upper part of my body feel like fire, and the lower part of my body feel like ice?"

The doctor began to wish that they had not met. She was sure that he was teasing her, but he had such a charming manner that she found it impossible to be angry and could only smile. For a third time she tested him, and yet again found nothing at all wrong with him.

"And what," she said laughing, "can I give someone who is not ill?"

"Noble lady, your gamcha!" Gesar pointed at the hat.

The doctor laughed disbelievingly, then impulsively took it from her head and gave it to Gesar.

Gesar called down the blessings of the gods on the doctor, for now he had another of the treasures of Guru Rinpoche.

Swallows wove an invisible pattern in the limpid blue sky above the few remaining competitors in the race for the throne of Ling. Gesar knew that not only the swallows looked down from the heavens, as he urged on his horse, for he was well up with the leaders in the race.

As they rode through a narrow ravine the high cliffs, eroded by wind and rain into patterns like the faces of strange beings, looked down upon them intently, broodingly. Gesar gained on the leaders. As the sound of his horse's hooves thundered in his ears, and seeing the cliffs, he thought for a second of how he had seen rock, stone harder than he could imagine, worn away by the gentle caress of water. As the riders emerged from the ravine Gesar overtook most of the leaders. There were now only two competitors ahead of him and the leader was Tondon's son Dutsum. The three men pounded across the fields surrounding the town of Ling as they neared the finish. Suddenly Gesar saw Dutsum's horse appear to stumble, then fall headlong. Dutsum managed to roll aside and avoid being crushed. Within seconds he was on his feet but a glance at his horse told him that while it was not seriously injured he could not continue on it. Dutsum drew his dagger and raced toward the oncoming rider, just ahead of Gesar.

"Stop. I am Dutsum, the steward's son. I order you to stop."

The rider slowed, undecided whether to stop, and as he came up to Dutsum, the young man, though of a portly build like his father, leaped at the rider, throwing him from his horse. Then Dutsum was in the saddle, urging the horse on to Ling, glancing back to see how close Gesar was. To his horror he saw that Gesar had stopped and was walking toward his injured horse, dagger drawn, with the evident intent of slitting its throat. Dutsum hesitated, but he could not ride on, he loved his horse too much. Turning back, he galloped towards Gesar. "Stop, Gesar! Please do not kill my horse!"

At that moment, while Dutsum was shouting, Gesar on the "horse of the gods," galloped into the market place, to the delight of the crowd, which went delirious with excitement. Dolma wept with joy and cried out from the top of the temple steps "Gesar! Gesar of Ling!"

Gesar was carried to the steps by the crowd—their hero, the child of the gods, the banished young prince, for it was said by many that the nomad boy was the natural son of the late king. He had proved his right to his inheritance by winning the race.

"Gesar! Gesar of Ling! Gesar! Gesar of Ling." The cry echoed through the town as he was hailed by the people.

Gesar ordered the crowd to part and led his horse to a water trough, then, surrounded by the chanting crowd, he loosened its girth and saw that a palace servant would look after the horse. Slowly he mounted the steps of the temple. He embraced Dolma and then Gongmo to wild cheers from the crowd. The head lama of the temple then assisted him to mount the throne of Ling. The royal robe was put around his shoulders, and he accepted the symbols of sovereignty as the monastic trumpets and the great drum were sounded. Gesar stepped down from his throne and helped Dolma onto the queen's throne. The crowd's welcome for their new queen was as warm as for their new king.

One of the first to enter the market place after Gesar was Tondon. Just outside Ling he had come across his son by his ailing horse, and had learned how Gesar had used a phantom body to trick Dutsum into turning back. Tondon was helped off his horse. The crowd was noisy, and not very friendly toward the steward. His buck teeth worked up and down as, panting for breath, the overweight steward climbed the temple steps toward the throne. Tondon paused before Gesar and the two looked at one another. Gesar smiled. Tondon laughed, and felt very relieved. He stepped forward.

"Nephew!" Tondon bowed low, and this public acceptance of Gesar drew cheers from the crowd.

Tondon draped a six-foot-long kata over the throne, then turned to the crowd in the market square.

"Today we have a new king. Ling Gesar!"

Amidst the cheers flintlocks exploded, and countless juniper incense fires were lit in thanksgiving as Tondon presented Dolma.

"The queen of Ling."

Gesar smiled at Dolma. A beautiful rainbow formed in the sky over the town. Gesar caught sight of the treasures on the table before him, the whip, the bow, the quiver, the hat. All were to play a part in his adventures, for Ling Gesar knew that in reality his story had just barely begun.

THE CASTLE IN THE LAKE

I N THE LAND OF TIBET, there was a beautiful lake surrounded by hills and mountains. So beautiful and clear was the lake that people who passed by would gasp in wonderment. Some would say that when the sun was high in the sky, casting the shadows of the mountain peaks across the calm expanse of water, it looked just as if there was a castle in the lake, a castle of such vast proportions that it filled the water. So the lake soon came to be known as "The Castle Lake."

Many stories grew up around the lake and its castle. Sometimes it was said that when the moon shone full and the stars gleamed like diamonds on the water, people could be seen rising from the lake, strange people, with eyes of fire and flowing hair hanging like wet leaves around their faces. Or fiery dogs would appear to tear the flesh from lone travelers walking the beach in innocence.

But, as is often the case with legends, father told daughter and mother told son through many generations, until the stories grew bigger and bigger with each telling, and finally they conveyed much more than the original teller intended. Soon it was generally accepted that there was indeed a castle in the lake, and that the castle had a king. The king, it was said, had many retainers, men who by some misfortune had fallen into the lake, or who had been captured while walking alone on its shores and were thereafter forced to remain in the service of the king.

One day a young herdsman was tending his yaks on the eastern side of the lake. Feeling a need for refreshment, he left his herd and made his way down to the water's edge. After he had splashed the cooling water onto his face, he lay back against a large rock, took his cheese and barley bread from his bag, lit a small fire to heat up his butter tea, and began to have his lunch.

While he was eating, Rinchen began to reflect upon his life. His mother was a cruel woman; she forced him to work hard so that she could buy new clothes and eat well, while he had to be content with a few cast-off rags and the scraps of food his mother did not want. Thinking thus, Rinchen began to cry. The tears rolled down his cheeks and sobs shook his body; he could work no harder and yet his mother wanted more and more.

As the boy began to pack away his things he looked up and saw a man standing at the water's edge. The man was tall and dressed in a black chuba dripping with water, looking just as if he had come up out of the lake. Recalling the stories he had heard about the Castle Lake and the king's retainers, Rinchen began to panic, and was just starting to run away when the man spoke.

"Why do you cry so?" the man asked. Rinchen turned to the man and saw that his face was gentle and kind, and heard that his voice was soft and melodious. All fear seemed to leave his body and he walked toward the tall man standing in the shallows of the lake. The man repeated his question and Rinchen told him about his mother and how she forced him to work harder and harder in order to keep her.

"Come with me into the lake," the man said, "for the king is a kind man and may be able to help you with your problem." The young herdsman felt fear begin to well inside him once more, for he was sure that if he went into the lake he would never return. The tall man sensed the boy's fear but in gentle tones which fell like music on the ear, he persuaded the young herdsman that he need not fear for his life.

"I am one of the king's retainers," said the man. "I will take you to see him and see that you return safely." The young herdsman thought for a moment, "What have I to lose?" "My mother is so cruel that even death would be better than spending the rest of my life in her bondage." And so, throwing his fear away, Rinchen followed the king's retainer into the lake.

The water was warm and friendly, and the boy was surprised that he could breathe quite freely. The king's retainer asked him to close his eyes as he led the boy through the water to the castle. When they stopped and Rinchen opened his eyes he saw that he was standing in a large hall, elaborately decorated in gold, shining silver, and beautiful shell. At the end of the hall was a throne, and on the throne sat an old man, the king.

The king beckoned to the boy to come forward and as he did so Rinchen noticed that he was not alone in the room with the king and his retainer, for standing on each side of the throne were more retainers, dressed in black chubas just like the tall man who met him on the shore of the lake. When he reached the foot of the king's throne, one of the retainers sprang forward and placed a small stool in front of the throne for the boy to sit on. Nervously, Rinchen sat down and looked up into the watery blue eyes of the king.

"Why do you come here?" asked the king in a deep voice which resembled the distant rumblings of thunder. The boy told the king his story, just as he had related it to the retainer on the shores of the lake.

The king listened, and when Rinchen had finished his story, he turned toward his group of retainers and motioned for one of them to come to him. The retainer approached the king and bent low while the king whispered instructions into his ear. The young herdsman strained but could not hear what the king was saying. The retainer left the hall and returned a few minutes later with a dog.

"Take this dog," said the king to the young herdsman, "but take care that you feed it before you feed yourself; that is very important." Rinchen took the dog, and with eyes closed let himself be led to the shores of the lake. When he opened his eyes he was alone with the dog.

The young herdsman went home with the dog and from that day on everything he desired appeared before him. He would wake up in the morning and find that barley had been placed in the barley chest, butter in the butter chest and money in the money chest. Even new clothes appeared in his clothes chest. He was very happy and always took great care of the dog, heeding the king's instructions to always feed it before feeding himself.

Rinchen's mother was amazed that her son should suddenly become so wealthy, and one day she decided to go out with the herd of yaks to see if she could discover the source of infinite plenty. While his mother was out of the house the young herdsman decided to watch the dog, for he was curious and wanted to know how the animal managed to produce the money and food. Hiding himself in the house, he watched the dog as it entered the door, walked over to the hearth, and violently began shaking itself.

Suddenly, the dog's skin fell to the ground, revealing a beautiful woman, the most beautiful woman Rinchen had ever seen. The woman went to the barley chest, opened the lid, and placed in it the barley, which appeared from nowhere. Then she did the same with the butter chest, the tea chest, the money chest, going all about the house producing everything that the boy and his mother needed.

Rinchen could contain himself no longer. He seized the dog's skin and threw it into the fire. The beautiful woman begged him not to do so, but it was too late, the skin burned quickly and was soon just a pile of ashes. Frightened that the chief's son would see the woman and take her for his wife, Rinchen covered her face with soot to hide her beauty, and kept her in the house away from the eyes of the people.

Soon, the young herdsman grew very rich, and with his wealth he grew exceedingly bold. "Why do I worry," he thought, "I have much money; the chief's son will not dare to steal the woman from me, for I can buy weapons and men." Thinking this, Rinchen washed the soot from the beautiful

74

woman's face and took her into the town to show her to the people, for he was very proud of her beauty.

The chief's son was in the town and saw the woman. He was determined that she should become his wife, and sent his men to fetch the woman to him. The young herdsman was distressed and called upon the men of the town to help him, but they were too afraid of the chief and his son, and not one man would come forward to help Rinchen save his woman.

Feeling very sad, the young herdsman went down to the shore of the lake, sat down by the large rock and began to cry. Just as before, the king's retainer appeared. "Why do you weep this time?" he asked. "I have lost my woman," the boy replied and told the whole story of how he had burned the dog skin and kept the beautiful woman hidden from the eyes of the people by covering her face in soot, but growing bold he washed her face, showing her beauty to the chief's son, and so lost her forever.

The retainer asked Rinchen to follow him into the lake again, for the king needed to be told the story. "Perhaps," said the retainer, "the king may be able to help you again." The young herdsman soon found himself in front of the throne once more at the feet of the king of the lake. After he heard the story of how Rinchen had lost the beautiful woman, the king gave him a small wooden box.

"Take this box," the king said, holding it out to the young herdsman. The boy took the box from the king. "Now," the king continued, "go to the top of a high hill and call the chief's son to war. When he has assembled his armies at the base of the hill, open the box and shout 'Fight!'" This the young herdsman did, and when he opened the box and called "Fight!" thousands of men charged out of the box and defeated the chief's son's soldiers.

Rinchen won back his beautiful woman and took her for his wife. He also took half of the chief's lands and became a rich, benevolent leader of the people. The young herdsman also returned the box to the king of the lake, thanking him and living in fruitful contact with him for all of his life.

THE YOUNG MAN WHO REFUSED TO KILL

ONCE THERE WAS A YOUNG MAN named Tashi who was not very skilled in the ways of the world. Try as he might the young man's father could not make him hunt for food—the son would refuse to take a life, and would not even eat the meat that his poor father brought home for the family pot.

Tashi had three sisters, all of whom had married rich men, and often his father and mother would lament their bad luck for having been left with a son who would not be able to take care of them in their old age, a son who would not hunt for game or fowl and who was so meek and mild in his ways.

"He should have been a monk," his mother would cry, "for what good is he to us, this son of ours? When we are old we will have to beg from our daughters and neighbors to save us from starvation." Such was his parents' constant plaint, but still the boy refused to take a life. "All life is sacred," he would say. "I cannot kill another living being."

One day Tashi's father insisted that the boy accompany him on a hunting trip. They walked for many miles and the father was getting very weary for it was a poor day and all he had managed to catch was a small rabbit. The father thought, "It is this son of mine; he brings bad luck."

The young man was sitting on a rock eating his meager ration of fruit and cheese and carving the prayer of Chenrezik into the rock beside him: OM MANI PADME HUM. All along the

76

path there were similar prayers carved into the rocks by travelers, for the path led up to a holy shrine which would be visited by travelers as they passed on their way. Chenrezik, the patron saint of Tibet, Lord of Compassion, commanded a great devotion from the people, and even Tashi's father, when he saw what his son was doing, silently mouthed the powerful prayer over and over again, moving the worn beads of his rosary through his fingers as he did so. Taking life was against his Buddhist beliefs, but he had to provide his wife with food, and he did try to kill the animals as humanely as possible, praying for them as he did so. It was plain to the father that he would never make his son see sense, the boy would never take a life, no matter how hungry they were, and he could see no way out of the situation.

Father and son walked on a little further, the father keeping a watch out for small animals and birds. Suddenly, through the trees, the father saw a sight that made him catch his breath. There in the field that bordered their path he saw a large hare. It was indeed the best thing that had come his way for many a week, and he was determined not to miss it. Taking up his sling the father crept through the trees to get a better view of the large brown animal. The hare was running toward them, his powerful hind legs pushing him forward at such a rate that it was impossible for the father to get a clear aim.

Suddenly, the hare stopped, as if sensing that there was danger. He twitched his nose, turned his head from side to side, and pricked his ears, listening. He was so near now that the boy could see the hare quite clearly, and so could his father who was just ready to send a large stone flying from his sling when the boy stood up and shouted, "No father, no; do not kill him!" The hare leaped into the air and was gone in a second, running for cover into a barley field which provided welcome refuge from his angry assailant.

The father stood spellbound for a few minutes, his face had turned ashen white and anger surged through his body. "Why?" he said to his son. "Why did you do that?" Tashi felt uncomfortable, he knew that his father was angrier than he had ever seen him before and that he could probably expect the beating of his life.

The father could control himself no longer. Taking a large rock from the side of the pathway he walked toward his son. "I will kill you," he said, "I will kill you, my only son." So saying, the father made to throw the rock at Tashi's head, but he backed away, frightened now and pleading with his father to spare his life. Just on one side of the path was a rocky incline, and on the side of the slope was a small cave. The opening was just a small crack and the young man backed toward it, just managing to squeeze himself into the cave before his father sent the rock hurtling toward his head. The rock struck his leg and he screamed out in pain.

Once inside the cave Tashi knew he was safe, since the opening was far too small for his father to enter. Tashi could not tell how large his rocky prison was, for it was dark and very difficult to see inside the cave. Inching his way along one of the jagged walls he reached the end of the cave just a few yards away from the entrance, and there, his leg pouring blood, he lay down and soon lapsed into unconsciousness.

It was many hours later when Tashi, roused into consciousness by the sound of footsteps, sat up and painfully recalled the events that had led up to his being injured and seeking refuge from his angry father. The footsteps grew louder. He called out for help, but his voice was weak and only a feeble whisper left his lips. Mustering all the energy he could, Tashi called again, this time louder. The footsteps stopped and he could hear voices softly murmuring outside the cave.

Suddenly, a head appeared at the opening, two eyes peered in at him and a voice shouted for him to come out of the cave. "I cannot move," he replied. "I am injured and find it difficult to move the few yards to the opening of the cave."

The head disappeared and was soon replaced by another. Then a small robed body maneuvered itself through the crack and crawled along the cave to Tashi. He could see that it was a monk moving toward him with outstretched hands to support him and lead him to safety. Once outside the cave Tashi saw that there were three monks, traveling together on pilgrimage to the holy shrines.

They carried him to a soft bank of grass, set him down and tended to his leg. Then, after sharing their food with him the monks asked Tashi to tell them his story, how he had come to be in such a sorry situation. The boy related his tale, telling them about his unwillingness to hunt for food, and how finally his father, driven to despair, had tried to kill his only son.

They carried him to a soft bank of grass, set him down and tended to his leg.

The monks listened without speaking; then the head monk invited the boy to accompany them on their travels. This he did, dressed in the robes of a mendicant monk.

After a few days they came to the house of Tashi's eldest sister. The head monk approached the door, knocked, and when the sister appeared, asked for alms. The sister went to fetch food for the wandering monks, but just as they were leaving she asked, "Have you seen my lost brother on your travels?" "He has been missing for many days and we are worried about him."

The head monk replied that they had not met with her brother on the way, but if they did they would surely tell him of her concern. The eldest sister did not recognize her brother dressed in the robes of a monk.

Soon they came upon the house of the young man's second sister. Once again the head monk approached the house and asked for alms, which he was given, and once again he was asked whether or not they had met with the lost brother. The head monk replied that they had not met with the young man and they went on their way.

When they came to the house of Tashi's youngest sister to ask for alms she immediately recognized her lost brother and hugged him, begging him to stay with those who loved him.

The three sisters gathered at the youngest sister's house and a feast was held to celebrate Tashi's return. The monks were given many gifts and were asked to stay as guests for as long as they pleased, but they declined and left the youngest sister's house to resume their travels.

Tashi thanked his sisters for their help and concern, but asked them to give him their blessings for he wanted to leave and make a life of his own. The sisters were sad to see their only brother go out into the world, and they gave him a gift of a magic horse which could speak. Tashi took the horse and made his way toward the remote regions of the land.

Before he had gone very far Tashi came to a vast plain. The horse spoke to him. "Kill me," he said. "Put my skin on the plain and scatter my hair all around so that the wind will carry it to the far corners of the plain."

The young man was horrified and refused to kill the horse. Instead he set down his pack, ate the food his sisters had given him, and prepared to rest for the night. During the night the horse threw himself over a steep precipice and was instantly killed.

When Tashi woke the next morning he looked for the horse, but he was nowhere to be seen. Searching all over the plain the young man came to the precipice, and peering down saw the shattered body of the horse. Feeling a great sadness and thinking of their conversation the night before, Tashi decided to do what the horse had asked. He took the skin, spread it out in the center of the plain, then scattered the horse's hair all around, throwing it up in the air so that the wind caught it and carried it to the farthest corners of the plain.

Instantly, the horse's skin became a huge mansion, and the hair became herds of sheep and yaks, grazing on the plain as far as the eye could see. The horse appeared before the boy and spoke once more. "You have shown only compassion toward other living beings; this is your reward." As soon as he had spoken the horse galloped off into the distance and disappeared. The young man noticed that where the horse's hooves had touched the ground little patches of gold appeared.

Looking around his new home, Tashi thought about his parents and wondered how they were managing to survive. He decided to go and see them and bring them home to live with him in the mansion. "My father and mother will never want for food again," he thought.

Tashi dressed in monk's robes again, for he did not want his parents to know of his new-found wealth, then he packed two bread pancakes and made his way to his parents' home. He climbed onto the roof of their house, peered down through a small window and saw his mother and father crouched in front of the fire. Tashi threw down a bread pancake. His mother seized it, declaring, "Gifts from heaven." The father snatched it from her and began to eat greedily. Tashi threw down the second pancake for his mother.

Then Tashi climbed down from the roof and knocked on the door of his parents' house. His mother answered and immediately recognized her son. Taking him in her arms she hugged him and begged him not to leave them again. The young man's father, too, was overcome with emotion and asked his son's forgiveness.

Tashi told his parents about his new home and his wealth and took them with him to the mansion on the plain. There he set his mother on a throne of purest gold, his father on a throne of purest silver, and he, their only son, sat on a throne of the pinkest shell.

NOTE: A Tibetan will sometimes purchase an animal from a butcher, and it will be allowed to live out its natural life, wearing a red woolen collar to show its special status. The owner believes this meritorious act may go a little way toward balancing out the often repeated unmeritorious act of eating meat. In a cold climate where meat production is easy and the growing of crops and vegetables can be difficult, meat was one of the staples of the Tibetan diet. But Tibetans did not delude themselves as to its incompatability with Buddhist teachings on harmlessness to all living creatures. Hence the often repeated invocation: "If an animal's flesh be eaten by one of merciful mind it will be led on the road of pure and perfect mercy" (in future lives). Being human though, Tibetans have frailties of nature, as do all of us, so the popular attitude is that the main responsibility lies with the butcher!

THE WHITE ROOSTER

I N THE SHADE OF A MOUNTAIN, by the side of a calm
lake, surrounded by all the beauty and loveliness of
nature, stood a small house. It was like a tiny jewel set
between mountain and lake, nestling in the subtle green and
brown shades of the grass and trees.

This spot was one of the prizes of nature, showing in its
character all the temperament of the seasons: the calm laziness
of summer, reflecting hazy shadows in the mirror-like lake;
the mellow thoughtfulness of autumn, when the trees come to
rest, dropping their leaves in yawning anticipation of winter's
sleep; the cruel beating of winter, as it wages war with weapons
of snow, ice, and wind, finally resting to view the conquered
land, lying silent beneath a gentle cover of snow; and beneath
this the earth nurtures the fresh youth of spring, waiting to
stretch its arms and meet the new dawn of life. The little house
saw the passing of the seasons, spring following winter, autumn
following summer; the lake gazed at the mountain; and the
mountain, in all its magnificent glory, looked protectively
down onto the little house and the lake as a father regards his
children, offering shelter and comfort.

The people who lived in the house also reflected the seasons. The mother, widowed, in the winter of her years, had
known the joys of youth, of falling in love, of giving birth to
three daughters, and now she wished only for their future
happiness. The eldest daughter, Pema, possessed a deep, haunt-

83

ing beauty, her eyes reflecting the burnished richness of deep autumn gold. The second daughter, Tsokyi, was like the summer, warm and beautiful, with a gaiety that surrounded her life with laughter and contented happiness. The family was poor, but this did not worry the second daughter, for she delighted in the simplicity of life and found joy in the meanest of tasks. The youngest daughter, Dekyi, was like the spring, fresh, innocent, and full of youthful energy, but unlike her second sister, she worried about her family's future, and dreamed of the day when they would all be rich and prosperous. So lived the family, in the little house, on the edge of a lake, overlooked by the snow-topped mountain.

Each day, in turn, one of the daughters would go out with the small herd of yaks to graze them on nearby pastures, while the other girls stayed at home to help their mother churn milk, roast barley, and attend to all the household chores. The herd of yaks was the family's only valuable possession. They milked the yaks to make butter and cheese; butter was used to fuel the lamps that illumined the home, and was also added to tea mixed with salt, thereby making a thick soup-like liquid that was both refreshing and nourishing to drink. Butter and cheese could also be traded for other essentials such as barley, salt, and household items. So the herd of yaks was most important to the family's well-being, and the daughters looked after them with much love and care.

One day, while Pema was out with the herd in a pasture, she became distracted by a loud crowing noise in the distance. As this was most unusual in such a remote spot, the girl left the herd to investigate the noise, but before she had gone very far, the noise stopped. Thinking that it was all in her imagination Pema returned to the meadow only to find, to her horror, that her yaks had disappeared! Feeling most distressed she searched high and low for the herd, but nowhere could they be found, nor could she hear the familiar lowing sound that the animals made. Thinking that they must have roamed farther afield, the girl began to widen her area of search, walking in unfamiliar surroundings but all to no avail.

Just as she was about to return home to break the news to her family, Pema spied, set in the side of a rock beside a narrow, rough-hewn path, a tiny red door. She walked up to the door and listened carefully, pressing her ear to the narrow gap of an opening. No sound came from within, so she pushed the door open just a crack, and looked inside. What she saw made her gasp in wonderment, for there, on the walls of the cave, were many precious jewels. Turquoise, amber, and emeralds glinted in the shaft of sunlight that entered the cave from the open door. Pema, losing all sense of caution, pushed the door wide open and entered the cave to look closer at the precious gems. Just as she was about to reach out and touch the large chunk of turquoise before her, she froze with fear, as a loud crowing noise echoed through the cave, rebounding off the low walls, then finally dying into a ghostly whisper.

When the noise stopped, Pema turned to look further into the cave. She squinted her eyes in the dimness, and could just make out a large brocade-covered throne at the end of the cave, and above the throne, encrusted with more jewels, hung a beautiful canopy.

The girl moved toward the throne, and as she did so she saw, hidden by the shadow of the canopy, a large white rooster. The rooster scratched his feet on the velvet cushion which was supporting him, yawned, cocked his head from side to side and moved forward a little so that the girl could now see him quite clearly.

"Hello," the rooster said, in dulcet tones. Pema was so astounded at the sight of a white rooster sitting on a throne that she was not at all surprised to find that he could also talk! "Hello," she replied. Neither spoke for some minutes, both just looked at one another, each waiting for the other to strike up conversation. Finally the rooster spoke again. "What are you doing here?" he asked.

Pema proceeded to tell him of her awful predicament, how she had heard his crowing and left her herd to investigate, only to find them gone when she returned to the meadow. "Perhaps you can help me find them," she said, thinking that this was no

"I will help you find the herd if you will consent to be my wife," the rooster said.

ordinary rooster. "I can certainly help you find your herd," said the rooster, "but what will I get in return for my help?"

Pema was silent for a while, and then she replied, telling the rooster that she came from a very poor family and could not offer gold or jewels, but would give him anything they owned if it would be of use. "Very well," the rooster said. "I will help you find the herd if you will consent to be my wife—you are not without beauty and I am sure you will make a good wife." Pema was dumb-struck; be the wife of a rooster, was his mind crazed! "I can do no such thing," she blurted, "I cannot marry a bird." "But I am no ordinary bird," the rooster said, "I will make you very happy."

The girl pleaded with the rooster but he still insisted that if she wished him to help her find the yaks, she must consent to be his wife, and the more the girl reasoned, the more stubborn the bird became, until, weary with pleading, Pema left the cave and made her way home to tell her family the news.

When she reached home, she fell into her mother's arms, burst into tears, and told of the lost herd and the strange rooster. The other daughters gathered round to try and comfort

86

her, but the evening was spent in despair as they all tried to think of a solution to their problem. Finally, it was decided that the next day Tsokyi would go out to look for the yaks, and if she could not find them, she too would approach the rooster and beg for his help. But as darkness descended, enveloping the house in blackness, the weight of unhappiness fell heavily on their hearts and sleep proved an impossible release from the problem.

Next morning, instead of greeting the day with happy anticipation, the family went about their tasks with little ease. Tsokyi took leave of her family, forcing a smile and trying to console them with the fact that she would soon be home with the herd. "Do not worry," she said. "The rooster will see reason; he will not be without compassion for a poor family." But even as she spoke a cloud covered the sun, casting deep gloom over the house and surrounding countryside.

Tsokyi followed her sister's footsteps of the previous day, searching the pasture land, listening for the sound of the herd in the hope that she would find them before reaching the little red door set in the side of the rock. But no herd appeared, and no sound reached her ears, it was as if the herd had disappeared from the face of the earth. There was nothing to do but visit the rooster, so Tsokyi, following her sister's instructions, made her way to the cave where he lived. Soon she found the door, tapped gently, and entered. The rooster was clearly visible on his throne at the end of the cave, and he continued to peck corn from a small silver bowl as he beckoned her to come forward by raising and waving one of his large pink legs. Such a strange sight made Tsokyi feel rather apprehensive, but very slowly and cautiously she moved toward the throne.

"Are you the rooster who spoke to my sister yesterday?" she asked. "If it was about the herd of yaks, yes I am," the rooster replied. "I have come to ask you to help us find the herd," said the girl, and she stared at the rooster with an unmoving gaze.

The rooster frowned, wrinkling the small feathers on his forehead, shifted himself uncomfortably on his velvet cushion, then met the girl's unwavering gaze with his own steely small eyes. "Will you be my wife?" the bird asked. Though secretly he thought he could not abide living with such a person who could look into the very soul of a being, he turned his eyes from hers and waited for the girl to answer.

"No, I will not be your wife, the thought is absurd," Tsokyi answered. "But I do ask you to show mercy to a poor unhappy family." The rooster watched the girl for a few minutes, shook his head, and said: "No wife, no yaks, and that is the end of the matter! I will not budge." The girl could see that her argument was useless, he was just a stubborn, willful rooster and was not going to be easily persuaded. "Very well then," she said, "if you will not help us to find the herd I will take some of your jewels instead."

So saying, Tsokyi reached out and snatched a large chunk of amber which rested on a rock near her feet. Just as she touched it a flash like lightning filled the cave, and when it subsided the jewels, the throne, and the rooster had disappeared! Feeling wretched, Tsokyi made her way back to the little house where her family was waiting to hear her news.

That night, the mother's heart was full of fear. They might never see their yaks again, and that would mean certain starvation for the family. Taking her youngest daughter's hand in her own, the old woman stroked the young flesh gently and asked Dekyi to visit the rooster the next day.

"You are as young as springtime," the old woman said to her daughter. "The rooster cannot refuse to help you, you are our last chance." The youngest daughter agreed to go and try to reason with the rooster, but in her heart she knew that her chances of persuading him to help them were not good. "If my two elder sisters failed," she thought, "I do not think the rooster will listen to me."

Next day, as Dekyi said goodbye to her family, the sun was shining on the mountain peak, making the snow appear red as fire. The mountain reflected in the lake, and the lake appeared to swallow up the mountain. "So great is the lake's love for the mountain," Dekyi thought, "it sees its changing faces, smiles with it, cries with it, reflecting in its own depths every changing mood of the mighty mountain. If the lake can swallow the mountain," thought the girl, "then my heart is not too small to accept all the sorrow of my mother and sisters. I must do what is best for them." Thinking this, she made her way to the cave to confront the rooster.

On reaching the door she knocked gently, but as no answer came from within the cave, she pushed open the door and entered. It was just as her sisters had described, the precious jewels, the richly decorated throne, and on the throne, sitting erect and looking tremendously large, was the white rooster. "You have come about the yaks," the rooster said, and the girl noticed that his voice was beautiful and melodious. "Yes," the girl replied, "I have come about the herd." "Well, you no doubt know the terms," the bird whispered, leaning over the side of the throne until his beak almost touched Dekyi's ear. "Only if you will be my wife will I help you to find the herd."

The girl lowered her gaze and replied, "Well, if those are your terms, I have no choice but to accept them; my family will starve without the yaks." As she spoke, two large tears fell from her eyes and rested on her youth-fresh cheeks. "More precious than all these jewels," said the rooster casting his eyes around the cave, "are your two crystal tears, for they are given out of true love for your family; you will indeed make a worthy wife." Then the rooster told the girl where she would find the yaks, and told her to return to the cave before sunset.

Following the rooster's instructions, Dekyi found her herd. She was so delighted to see them again that she forgot her sorrow and ran to them, hugging and calling each of them by name; then she led them home to her anxiously waiting family.

On reaching home, Dekyi remembered her promise and began to make ready to leave the family she loved and go to live with the strange rooster. The mother was distressed when she learned of her daughter's sacrifice, and begged her not to leave. Pema pleaded with Dekyi, saying that she would go in her place, and Tsokyi did likewise. But Dekyi refused their offers of help saying, "He is not a bad rooster, really, he is kind I am sure, and has a soft voice which is like music to the ears; I will be well cared for." And so saying she bade farewell to her weeping mother and two sisters. As she left, Dekyi did not look back at the family, nor did she glance at the mountain and lake, for tears were in her eyes and she did not wish to show her distress.

Sometime later, in a nearby town, the people were making ready for the annual horse races. This was a big event, and was attended by people from all the surrounding villages who came to see the country's most skilled horsemen perform feats of courage and endurance. It was also a time for merry-making and celebration and everyone revelled in the spirit of carnival time. The women dressed in their finest clothes, displaying their wealth by the amount of turquoise and coral in their elaborate headdresses, and the men tried to outdo their friends in games of archery, tests of strength, and dice playing. Soon, the big day arrived, tents were erected, feasts were prepared, and everybody gathered, determined to enjoy themselves. One young woman stood out from the rest of the crowd. She was so stunningly beautiful, so expensively dressed, that the other women gazed at her in envy. One woman even ventured to remark that she looked very much like the youngest daughter of the widow who lived by the lake, and on closer examination they found that it was indeed her. Much conversation surrounded her appearance. "She must have made a good match in marriage," the women agreed, but they all wondered why she attended the races alone, for every day the girl would turn up without a husband.

During the races there was one horse that far outclassed the others. He was most unusual, being an almost ice-blue color, and his rider was by far the most dashing of young men to compete in the events. Every day this unusual horse and rider were champions of the races, and every day both would disappear, never to be seen feasting and enjoying the festivities. Dekyi, too, wondered about this handsome young man, for she noticed that he always sought her gaze and smiled at her after winning a race.

On the last day of the festival, Dekyi offered to walk part
of the way home with an old woman and so she left the races
early. As they walked the old woman asked the girl about her
marriage, and why her husband did not accompany her to the
races. Dekyi told the old woman how she had become the wife
of a large white rooster to save her famiy from starvation, and
how her husband had persuaded her to attend the races even
though he did not want to go. The old woman sympathized with
the girl, telling her that she must not worry: "Do not be misled
by appearances," she said, "for things are not always what they
seem." Dekyi felt comforted by the old woman's words, and
after seeing her safely to her house she made her way back to the
cave.

On reaching the cave she looked for her husband, but he
was nowhere to be seen. Dekyi went outside and called to him,
but no answer came. Finally she decided to give up her search,
thinking that he must have attended the races after all, and she
went back into the cave to await his arrival. Just as she was
about to reach for the large teapot on the wrought-iron brazier,
Dekyi noticed a white skin lying on the floor in front of the fire.
She stooped to pick it up, and was horrified to discover that it
was the skin of her husband, the rooster. Dekyi sat down and
the events of the last few days passed through her mind. The
dashing young man on the strange blue horse who always
disappeared at the end of the races, the old woman telling her
that things are not always what they seem, and the way the
young man looked at her, with a look that was so familiar!
Seizing the skin, she threw it into the fire, and watched as the
flames consumed every part of it. "My husband is the young
man on the blue horse," she whispered to herself. "Now that I
have burned the rooster's skin we can live properly as man and
wife."

When the skin was nothing but ashes, and the flames of the
fire flickered and began to die, Dekyi went outside to fetch
more fuel. She heard the galloping of horse's hooves in the
distance and stood waiting for a glimpse of the rider. It was just
as she had thought: the ice-blue horse came galloping at high

speed down the narrow path with the young man looking flushed and excited on its back. He stopped outside the cave, and when he saw Dekyi standing there he immediately ran inside. "What have you done with my skin?" he shouted as he came rushing out again. "I have burnt it," the girl replied, "now we can live together as man and wife, and I will not have to live in shame of being married to a rooster." The young man looked dismayed. "You have made a big mistake, my wife," he said. "While I am able to return and live in the skin of a rooster I am safe and have good fortune, but without my skin I will become a slave of the demons."

His words frightened the young girl. "Why do you have to live in the skin?" she asked. The young man told her how he had become wealthy and lived in peace only by agreeing to become a slave to the demons. When he had rebelled and refused to be their slave the demons sentenced him to life as a rooster. He could only leave his skin for a few days each year, and if he did not return to it the demons would come and take him away.

"Husband, what can I do?" asked Dekyi. "There must be some way of stopping the demons from taking you." But the young man told her there was only one way to prevent the demons from coming. If she could sit by the door with a candle, day and night for a whole week, so heating the door to keep the demons from entering, then he would be free. Dekyi agreed to do this, and so she sat, day and night, night and day, forcing herself to stay awake so that the demons could not enter. On the last day, unable to keep her eyes open any longer, she fell asleep. The candle she was holding dropped to the floor and went out before her husband could reach it.

When Dekyi awoke her husband was gone, and she knew that the demons had taken him away. Feeling sad, she went into mourning for her husband. "He must surely be dead," she told herself. "The demons will not have had mercy on him." She continued to live in the cave, feeling that since she had been the cause of her husband's death it was only right that she should pay penance for her foolish deed.

One day, while she was out walking, Dekyi came upon a man carrying wood. When she got closer to him she recognized him as her husband. She ran into his arms, thankful that he was alive. The husband told her that he was now a slave of the demons and could never return to her, but that she was not to worry for he was well. Then he persuaded her to go home to her family and take with her all the precious jewels that were in the cave. Dekyi returned home to her mother and two sisters. They were overjoyed to see her again, and with the jewels she was able to provide them with a life of luxury in which they would never want for anything.

And again the lake smiled at the mountain, and the mountain looked protectively down on the happy little house beside the calm mirror-like lake.

NOTE: The rooster on the weathervane of English country churches symbolizes the dawn of the sun of Christ dispelling the powers of darkness; in the Buddhist context the rooster symbolizes the sun, but he also represents pride and arrogance.

The Clever Mice

The mice are eating all the food!
They must be sent away,
We cannot kill, so we will ride,
For many a long day.
Old people laugh:
"They will come back,
They always do," they cry.
"How can you tell?" the young ones ask,
"The same to every eye?"

"We'll mark them with a daub of paint,
Bright red upon their back."
The mice are caught
And marked, each one,
Then carried in a sack.

A long, long ride,
The mice released,
The journey home is fast,
With peaks and rivers,
Dales and hills,
No mouse could ever pass.

The days go by, the young ones mock,
"Where are the little mice?"

THE CLEVER MICE

Three weeks have gone,
The table's laid, with tsampa and with meat,
A movement in the empty room,
The flash of tiny feet,
A grey shape climbs a table leg,
And lifts a tiny head,
A smell of food,
The whiskers twitch,
This mouse will be well fed.

The sharp teeth bite.
The mouse is joined
By others, weak and thin,
The same grey coats,
And bright black eyes,
Red daubs upon their skin.

NOTE: This is the sort of story that would be told in Tibet to explain the meaning of karma (cause and effect) to young children. The mice represent one's past deeds: no matter how one tries to escape them, despite all one's efforts to cover up, one will always have to face the consequences.

THE MONKEYS AND THE MOON

ONCE, IN THE DISTANT PAST, there was a band of monkeys. They lived in a forest, and in the forest was a well. One night, the leader of the band of monkeys peered into the well, and seeing the reflection of the moon in the water, said:

"Look! the moon has fallen into the well; we ought to get it out or our world will be without a moon."

The other monkeys looked into the well and saw that it was indeed so. "Yes," they agreed. "We should certainly get the moon out of the well."

So the monkeys formed a chain, each holding onto the tail of the one before, while the monkey at the top of the chain held onto a branch to support them.

The branch began to bend under the weight of the monkeys as they lowered themselves into the well, and soon began to crack. The water was disturbed and the reflection of the moon disappeared, the branch broke, and the monkeys tumbled headlong into the well.

WHEN THE UNWISE HAVE AN UNWISE LEADER
THEY ARE ALL LED TO RUIN.

FAVORITE VERSES,
PROVERBS, AND RIDDLES

There is no eye like understanding,
No blindness like ignorance,
No evil like illness,
Nothing so dreaded as death.

—Buddhist Precepts

One treasure, and one alone, can no robbers steal.
One treasure, and one alone, can one take through
the doors of death.
The wise man's wealth lies in good deeds that
follow ever after him.

—*Khuddakapatha*

Cling not to experiences:
Ever-changing are they.

—Phadampa Sangye

The three worlds are transitory, like an autumn cloud.
The birth and death of beings is like watching a dance.
The length of a being's life is like a lightning flash,
Coming swiftly and abruptly to an end,
Like water dashing over a steep precipice.

—The Four Contemplations

97

Finally obliged to depart, even a king cannot take his
　　wealth and companions along,
But wherever he goes or stays, the results of his actions
　　will follow him, inseparable as a shadow.
　　　　　　　　　　　　—The Four Contemplations

Rebellious thoughts are like an abandoned house
　　taken over by robbers.
　　　　　　　　　　　　—Phadampa Sangye

To cherish oneself brings only downfall.
　　　　　　　　　　　　—Guru Puja

The crow calls the hog black.

Gold lies deep in the earth, yet its light shines bright in the sky.
(Good deeds, although hidden, will always bring benefit.)

If gold is poured in the donkey's ear, he will shake it out.
If sand is poured in the donkey's ear, he will shake it out.
(The ignorant cannot tell the difference between what is
wholesome and unwholesome.)

One mouth, two tongues.
(Said of someone who is two-faced.)

Lazy in the morning, working late at night.

A rabbit cannot put his paws on the horns of a deer.
(Said of one who has aspirations beyond his capabilities.)

You can't get two taxes from one man;
You can't put two saddles on the same horse.

Having drunk the country's water, one should obey the
country's laws.

Better than the young man's knowledge is the old man's
experience.

If the inner mind is not deluded, then outer deeds will not
be wrong.

The life of every being is like a bubble in water.

Honor a king in his own land; honor a wise man everywhere.

Knowing just one word of wisdom is like knowing a hundred
ordinary words.

If one desires to have true happiness, one must be perfect
in suffering.

The wise pursue wisdom, the dull follow in blind faith.

If one is not learned, but pretends to know, it is evil.
If one is learned, but hides it within, it is evil.

There are three cold and three warm times in a spring day.
In a man's long lifetime, there are three joys and three sorrows.

It goes all over the world, but we cannot see it.
    [*The wind.*]

She eats all the best food and never gets fat.
    [*A saucepan.*]

It has two wings but cannot fly away.
    [*A scissors.*]

THE KIND MAN

ONCE THERE LIVED a very kind, generous man. He was admired and loved by many for his good works and kindly deeds. One day, a very famous lama came to his village. The man asked to speak with the famous lama, and when this wish was granted he prostrated himself at the feet of the holy man, and spoke to him thus:

"I would like to become an enlightened being, compassionate and wise, so that I may help all living beings, and devote my life to the teaching of the Buddha. What should I do?"

The lama saw that the man was sincere in his motives and told him to go to the mountains and spend his life praying and meditating. He gave the kind man a special prayer to chant, and told him that if he did this constantly and with great devotion, then he would surely become an enlightened being, able to help all others through his wisdom and compassion.

The man did as the lama instructed. He went into the mountains which surrounded the village, found a cave, and began to meditate in earnest. For many years he persevered, but still he did not become enlightened. After twenty years had passed, the famous lama visited the village again. The kind man heard of his arrival and went down from his mountain cave to seek an audience with the lama.

He waited for days while many people lined up to see the famous lama and get his blessing. Finally, he was allowed to see the holy man, and after he paid homage by prostrating three

101

times at the lama's feet, and by offering him a white scarf, the kind man told him of his plight.

"For twenty years I have been meditating and praying as you instructed," he said, "but still I am not enlightened. I must be doing something wrong."

The lama looked solemn.

"What did I tell you to do?" he asked the man.

The kind man told him everything he had been doing for twenty years.

"Oh," said the lama. "I'm afraid that is no use at all, I told you the wrong thing, you will never be enlightened now."

The kind man was shattered, he fell to the lama's feet and cried.

"I am sorry," said the lama, "there is nothing more I can do for you."

The kind man, who by now was quite old, felt that twenty years of his life had been wasted. He went back to his cave.

"What am I to do?" he thought. "For all these years I believed that I would become enlightened, now I have to abandon all hope of ever achieving that aim." He sat down on the stone slab, that for twenty years had been his cushion, bed, and table, crossed his legs, closed his eyes, and thought:

"I may as well carry on with my prayers and meditation, what else is there for me to do now?"

So without any hope of attaining enlightenment he began to meditate and chant the prayers that had become so familiar during his long retreat.

Immediately, he became enlightened.

He saw the world in all its reality, everything was clear. He understood, at last, that it was only his grasping at enlightenment that prevented him from attaining it. Now he would be able to help all living beings find peace through his wisdom and compassion. Now he would leave his cave and go back into the world to spread the teachings of the Buddha.

He walked out of his cave and gazed at the village below. He had seen it so often before, but never so clearly as now. For a moment he thought he heard the soft laugh of the famous lama, as he looked up at the sky and the huge rainbow which was stretching its arc across the snowy peaks.

NOTE: An illustration of the Tibetan belief that it is necessary to give up in order to attain. The lama uses "upaya," skillful means, to lead the kind man to enlightenment. Although the kind man was shocked and disappointed to learn his practice of twenty years was wasted, he carried on with his meditation. Having no further subtle aim, he achieved his goal. Less skillful teachers than the lama of this story have been known to try similar methods, only to find their students abandoning the practice altogether, thus defeating the objective. This emphasizes the necessity for a careful match between a skillful teacher and a receptive student.

In addition to presenting the lama with a kata (see the note on "Padmasambhava and the Felicity Scarf"), the kind man prostrated three times before the lama. A prostration is performed by touching the crown of the head, the throat, and the heart with joined hands, then sliding fully outstretched onto the floor. It is an act of homage to the lama who represents the Buddha, his teaching, and the assembly of enlightened beings. The gesture of joined hands toward the head, throat, and heart indicates the surrender of body, speech, and mind.

The title "lama" literally means "higher" or "superior one" and is the Tibetan translation of the Sanskrit term "guru." It is a title given to widely respected spiritual teachers. Although most lamas are monks, there are lamas of the married clergy and sometimes laymen who are addressed with this title because of their spiritual insight. The term is also customarily used to address very learned monks, those who hold official positions in a monastery, and the thousand or so officially recognized "incarnate lamas" or "tulkus" of whom the best known is the Dalai Lama. Incarnate lamas are believed to be great spiritual teachers who are reborn to continue their work, or who use someone as a channel for their power.

THE THREE DAUGHTERS
AND THE LOST COW

ONCE THERE WAS A FAMILY who owned a very special cow, it was black and white with horns of purest shell. One day, the family was distressed to find that the cow had disappeared, and search as they would, they could not find her. Now in the family were three daughters, and since they were all of responsible disposition they each went to look for the cow alone, thinking they would certainly please their parents by finding the lost beast.

The eldest daughter made her way to a nearby river, and meeting with an old hag, asked her, "Have you seen our lost cow?" The old hag, withered and worn with age, replied, "And what does she look like?" The girl described the cow to the old woman, but she answered that she had not seen the cow. The girl thanked the old hag, and was about to walk off in the direction of the forest, thinking that the cow might have gone into the shelter of the trees, when the old hag spoke again.

"Come across the river to my house," she invited, "Your cow may have strayed across the water." The eldest daughter went with the old woman, and when they reached her house was pleased to join the woman in a meal which was offered in a smooth silver-lined bowl. The girl ate heartily, not knowing that the old woman was feeding her pieces of human flesh.

Soon afterwards, the second daughter found her way to the river's edge, and she too met with the old hag. Asking her the same question about the lost cow, the old woman again replied that she had not seen it, but invited the girl to cross the river to her house. On reaching the house the old hag invited the girl to eat, placing in front of her a bowl of human flesh, which the girl ate with relish, not knowing what the dish contained.

Then, the youngest daughter, having searched high and low for the cow, made her way to the river. The old hag appeared, and the young girl asked, "Have you seen a black and white cow with horns of purest shell?" Once again, the old hag replied that she had not seen the animal, but invited the girl to cross the river with her.

The young girl went with the old hag to her small house. She noticed that it was shabby, and lacked the familiar things that made the difference between a house and a home. There was no large gleaming teapot steaming on the brazier, no little shrine in the living quarters. "But then," the girl thought, "the old hag may have a shrine in the adjoining room." But even as she looked toward the door that led to the other room, the girl realized that this was probably not so, for the door was barred and bolted.

The old hag offered the girl food, which she spooned from a large black pot and poured into the same smooth silver-lined bowl that the young girl's sisters had eaten from. The girl began to eat, but was offended by the smell of the food, for it had an unfamiliar odor. Just then, the old woman went into the yard to fetch wood for the fire. As she did so, the girl noticed a small dog crouched in the corner of the room. The dog approached the girl, and in soft tones, spoke to her, saying that if she would give him the remainder of her food he would tell her where the missing cow was.

The girl gave him the food which he ate greedily, and when he had licked the bowl clean he spoke again. "Your two sisters are locked in that room," he said, indicating the barred door. "So is your black and white cow with horns of purest shell." The girl was incredulous, so unbelievable was the statement, but then the dog's voice became urgent.

"Kill the old hag," he said, "She is a witch and means to do you harm." The seriousness of the dog's voice convinced the girl; she seized a large knife and waited behind the door for the old hag to enter. When the woman returned to the house, the girl let fly with the knife and chopped off her head. Then, unbarring the door, the girl tried to open it and set her sisters free, but it was firmly locked, and try as she might it would not budge. The little dog came to her rescue again—he sniffed in the old hag's apron pocket and emerged with the key to the door in his mouth.

The young girl unlocked the door and set her sisters and the cow free. Then the girls searched the house and found much gold and precious jewels which they took home with them, together with the black and white cow with horns of purest shell, and the little dog who had saved them from the cruel witch.

THE WEATHERMAKER

ONCE UPON A TIME there was a wise man. He traveled throughout the vast land of Tibet, stopping at villages and towns wherever his services were required. He could foretell the future, he could tell a family the most auspicious days for traveling or trading, he could even change the weather! The wise man was much admired, and people paid well for his services.

From his appearance one could be forgiven for thinking him poor, but the people who were acquainted with him certainly knew better. To hear him talk one could easily mistake him for a man with a crazed mind, but the people who called on him for help certainly knew better. This strange man, in his ragged robe, with a large double-sided drum and a skull cup hanging from his belt, was neither poor nor stupid. He was, some said, possessed of magical powers. These magical powers he used for the good of all beings, but, and this was the crux of the matter, if anyone dared to cross his path he could turn his magical powers to other uses, and so destroy all opposition. He was known to everyone as the Weathermaker.

If one could by chance see what was contained within the Weathermaker's chuba and bag, one would see many treasures, for he had no permanent home, carrying his belongings with him from village to village. To see him perform a ceremony was very awe-inspiring, and people would gather to watch, as the Weathermaker appeared to go into a trance-like state, banging his drum in ever-changing rhythms and making gestures with his free hand, summoning the power of the gods. He would sit for many hours, chanting in a low, deep voice that seemed to come from the very bowels of the earth, inviting the gods to shower their power and blessings upon the gathering. The Weathermaker's smile was like the sun, his whole face would light up, and his eyes reflected a warmth that one could not help but feel.

One day, after finishing a ceremony of blessing upon a household, the Weathermaker took the gifts of food that the family bestowed upon him, and proceeded to make his way to another village several days journey away. He was watched by a very large Hare, who with eyes full of greed and belly grumbling with hunger, gazed on the Weathermaker and his food with envy. "I will think of a way," he thought, "to rob the ragged rogue of his food," and so, with his mind busy on a plan, the hare followed the Weathermaker as he journeyed.

Before they had gone very far, the Hare heard a fluttering of wings and felt the light touch of feet on his back. It was a Magpie. "Hello Hare," the Magpie said. "Have you been able to find food?" "No," replied the Hare, "I am weak and hungry; food is very scarce." "I know, my friend," the Magpie said, "Let us travel together, maybe we will fare better." So, the Magpie flew into the air and followed the Hare on his travels.

Next day, the Hare and Magpie came upon a Fox. The Magpie became excited, dipping and soaring in the air. "The Fox looks very weak," said the Magpie to the Hare. "If he dies, we will be able to feast on fox meat." "Hello Fox," the Hare said, "Where are you going?" The fox lifted his head and spoke to the Hare, "I am very hungry," he said, "and so are my children, I am looking for food." "Come with us," invited the Hare, "we may do better if we travel together." And so, the Hare, the Magpie, and the Fox walked on together, but only the Hare knew that they were trailing the Weathermaker.

Eventually they reached a forest where the shade of the trees was soothing to the animals. The Magpie stopped to pick some berries from a small bush, but these did not appeal to the

Hare and Fox, who turned up their noses in disgust. Then, from behind a large tree, they spied the massive form of a Wolf. Petrified with fear, the Hare and the Fox froze where they stood, while the Magpie, screaming in terror, flew high into the sky and perched on the topmost branch of a tall tree. The Wolf, disturbed by the noise of the Magpie, turned, to be confronted by the frightened gaze of the other two animals. "Do not be frightened," the Wolf growled, "I am too old to kill." The Hare edged forward. "How do you eat if you cannot kill?" he asked. "That is a problem," the Wolf answered, "for I have children to feed." He looked sadly down at the ground. "I am not as swift and powerful as I used to be." "Come with us," invited the Hare, his huge brown eyes glinting with excitement. "I have a plan that may help us all." "And what is your plan?" said the Magpie, having left his place of security to join in the conversation.

"Well," said the Hare, "walking just ahead of us is a Weathermaker." "A Weathermaker!" the animals chorused. "How can he help us?" The Hare continued, "The Weathermaker is not a poor man," he said, "I have seen him put much food into his bags." At this the other animals suddenly became interested. "Now, what I suggest, is that you my friend," he said, pointing to the Fox, "lie in a ditch and pretend to be dead. The Magpie here will make a noise to bring the Weathermaker to you." The animals listened intently. "When he leaves his belongings to look at you, the Wolf and I, being the strongest, will steal his goods and run away." "What if he catches me and kills me?" the Fox asked, much preferring not to be the one left in the ditch. "He will not catch you," chirped in the Magpie. "You can jump over his back and run away." Reluctantly, the fox agreed to the plan. "But first," he said, "we must overtake the Weathermaker and none of us can run fast enough because we've had so little food."

The Hare thought for a while, and then he said, "The Weathermaker is going to the next village. Now, if we travel by river we will overtake him before he gets there." The animals made their way down to the river, and luckily for them, there was a large log floating near the bank. The Hare, Fox, and Wolf climbed onto the log, and were soon slicing through the water with increasing speed, while the Magpie flew overhead ready to signal to them as soon as they had overtaken the Weathermaker.

When the Magpie saw that they had passed far enough in front of the Weathermaker, he gave the sign for the animals to land. This proved to be no easy task, and they were forced to abandon the log and swim for the shore, an experience that the Hare could well have done without! Just as the Hare had planned, the Weathermaker, on hearing the cries of the Magpie, and seeing the bird hovering over a ditch, left his belongings and went to investigate. When he saw the Fox lying prone in the ditch, he thought it must be dead. "He has a fine coat," the Weathermaker thought, "I will skin him." Just as he reached into his chuba to bring out his knife, the Fox, unable to lie still a moment longer, leaped out of the ditch and was away.

When the Weathermaker, astonished, turned to watch the Fox in flight, he caught a glimpse of the Wolf and Hare as they disappeared into the distance carrying his belongings, being hotly pursued by the Fox and Magpie. When the animals felt that they were safe, they stopped to share the Weathermaker's belongings. The crafty Hare took charge of the proceedings, and to the Magpie he gave the Weathermaker's hat. To the Wolf he gave the Weathermaker's boots, and to the Fox he gave the large ritual drum, keeping all of the food for himself. The animals were so pleased with their new possessions that they did not realize they had been deceived by the cunning Hare, and they all went happily on their way, each clutching his ill-gotten gains.

All did not go well for the animals however. The Wolf, in his brand new boots, went hunting for sheep. Being unable to run fast in his heavy footwear, he tripped, and was nearly killed as the sheep trampled him.

The Magpie, in the big new hat that almost covered his body, sat under a Yak. The Yak let drop a huge yak-chip onto the hat, trapping the Magpie and nearly causing him to die of suffocation.

The Fox went home to meet his family, who were anxiously awaiting his return. On a bridge that crossed a racing river, the Fox's wife and children stood, ready to greet him. As he approached the bridge and saw his family waiting there, the Fox began to bang his ritual drum so loudly that his children threw themselves into the river in fright and were drowned.

Soon, the animals all met again. The Fox, the Magpie, and the Wolf all related to each other their tales of woe, but the Hare sat silently in the shade of a huge tree. After the animals had told their stories they all looked expectantly toward the Hare. The Hare spoke, "Friends," he said, "we made a grave mistake. The Weathermaker has magical powers, and by stealing his belongings we have brought misfortune upon ourselves. You all think that you have suffered, but look at me." So saying, the Hare moved from the shadow of the tree that had hitherto kept him hidden. "I too have suffered," he said, "for while eating the Weathermaker's food I split my lip." The animals gasped as they saw the split in the Hare's lip that reached right up to his nose! The Hare continued, "All beings," he said, "human or animals, who look on me, should be warned, that to do evil, brings only suffering upon oneself."

And to this day, after many generations, the Hare still bears the mark of its cunning ancestor.

THE DISRESPECTFUL SON

AT THE TIME WHEN the land of Ndu was ruled by a very strict and powerful king, there lived a poor widow, whose only means of support was her one son Dorje. He was full of rebellious thoughts and brought much trouble upon himself and his poor mother by his disrespectful ways. He would not bow to the command of the king, nor did he listen to the advice of the elders. He knew his own mind, and did not watch his tongue, always speaking foolishly. This caused the people of the kingdom to turn against him, for when the king was angered by the young man's actions, they all suffered. Eventually, Dorje was forced to abandon his mother, his lands, his possessions, and leave the land of Ndu, for the people were roused against him and many threatened to put an end to his life.

Carrying only the barest of essentials, the young man began his journey to strange unknown parts. As he walked he felt the comforting heaviness of the large amulet his mother had given him. The charm box contained many precious things: slips of paper with prayers and magical drawings; clay figures of deities; and most precious of all, a tiny zi bead. The zi bead was a highly prized possession, being able, it was said, to protect the wearer from injury.

Dorje walked wherever his fancy took him, caring not where his footsteps led. Crossing rivers and streams, hills and mountains, he continued with his journey. Soon however, his food ran out, and he was forced to subsist on wild berries, occasionally begging a little rice, cheese, or roasted barley from other travelers he met on the way. Food was hard to find, and often nighttime would find him cold and hungry, with only the vague comfort of a better tomorrow in his thoughts.

As the days passed, he grew increasingly weaker and found he could not walk as far or as fast as when he began. Finding himself on a high plateau, he looked in all directions to find the easiest way to travel. The country was wild and deserted. In the distance on one side Dorje could see the looming hostility of the mountains, perhaps thirty miles away, with nothing but rocky wilderness between.

In the other direction, however, was a wide rolling plain, ending in the gentle slope of green hills. The long grass of the plain looked infinitely more inviting than the rocky wilderness, so Dorje began his slow descent from the high plateau, heading for the flat plain, with its long grass, occasional expanse of dry dusty land, and few trees. He was struck by the extremes of climate and the weird, ever-changing scenery. This land was surely a strange land, and he felt pangs of apprehension stab in his stomach.

When he reached the plain, Dorje was drawn to a small black cloud just a few yards away. When he investigated he found that it was hordes of flies hovering over the dead body of a horse. The horse had not been dead for long, for the flies had made little impact on the body, and thinking that the horsemeat would make a hearty meal, the young man set about cutting off the horse's head with a large knife which he kept inside his chuba. It was a long task, but done without feeling of distaste, for his belly was groaning in anticipation of a satisfying meal. When Dorje had completed the job of cutting off the horse's head, he slung it over his shoulder and made for the shelter of a spreading tree, just visible in the distance. The low branches of the tree, he thought, would provide a suitable place to eat and rest for the night, for the sun was slowly beginning to disappear beneath the horizon and darkness would soon descend.

On reaching the tree, Dorje, with the horse's head still slung over his shoulder, climbed onto one of the lower branches and settled himself among the leaves. Darkness had fallen, swiftly and silently, as if a curtain had been drawn across the sky, a curtain painted with the ghostly glow of the silver moon which cast shimmering light over the surrounding land.

The young man, by now quite ravenous, began to tear at the horseflesh, eating it as if it were the nectar of the gods, so sweet was the taste of red meat to his long-starved taste buds. Something caught his eye . . . he looked up, startled, his eyes searching the landscape for a movement. Then, out of the shadow, clothed in the light of the moon, Dorje saw something that chilled his heart with fear and sent shivers of terror running up and down his spine. Flying toward him on wild horses, were the most terrible demons he had ever seen. Even in his darkest nightmares Dorje had never looked upon such ugly fearful beings.

He closed his eyes, hoping that the demons would pass, but the thundering hooves drew nearer, and the snarling, gnashing of teeth, and lashing of whips seemed to surround him. The demons stopped beneath the tree in which he crouched; he forced himself to open his eyes and look down onto the terrible spectacle below. The demons' faces were too ugly to be described, and their eyes, red and rolling in their sockets, looked this way and that, as if searching for intruders. Dorje hardly dared to breathe, but slowly he moved his head to his amulet, and clutching it in earnest he began mentally praying for protection.

The demons began to speak, voices barely audible gurgled from their blood-red lips and hissed in the night air. Dorje could just make out some of the conversation, the demons were saying that they lusted for the taste of human flesh! The young man's body now began to shake uncontrollably, he was unable to keep hold of the horse's head, and it fell from his grasp and landed right at the feet of the gathered demons. Shrieking and shouting, the demons scattered in all directions, believing that the horse's head had fallen from the sky and was an ill omen!

For what seemed hours, Dorje could not move, but eventually his body relaxed, as fear turned to relief, and he climbed down from the tree just as the sun was beginning to rise in the sky, throwing the welcoming light of dawn over the surrounding land. On the ground beneath the tree he noticed a golden bowl. Realizing that one of the demons must have dropped it in his hurry to escape, the young man was loath to touch the object. The gleam of gold, however, soon made him overcome his misgivings, and placing the bowl inside his chuba the young man continued on his way.

The distant green hills looked welcoming, but it seemed to Dorje that the faster he walked, the farther away they appeared to be. Finally, nearly collapsing with exhaustion, he sat down to rest awhile. In need of food, he emptied out his travelling bags in hope of finding some scrap of food, but there was not even the smallest morsel. He picked up the golden bowl and moaned in despair. "A bowl that golden gleams," he said to himself, "of precious metal made, and yet I would gladly swap this bowl for a small portion of plain rice." Then, shouting in anguish, he cried, "Oh, I do wish this bowl was full of food!" Just as the words were uttered the bowl immediately filled to the brim with food!

"A magic bowl!" he exclaimed, unable to believe his luck, and with tears of joy running down his cheeks he greedily ate the food. When Dorje had finished and licked the bowl clean, he asked for more food. This time he asked for all the delicacies he had yearned for during his long journey, and sure enough, the bowl produced the food. Dorje then asked for drink, which the bowl provided; as much as he asked for, the bowl magically produced.

Feeling refreshed, Dorje decided to experiment with the bowl, asking it to produce gold, silver, and precious gems, but the bowl did not respond, it would only fill with food or drink. "Never mind," he thought, "I will not be hungry or thirsty again," and so he continued on his travels.

Having reached the green hills and wandered into a sparsely populated valley Dorje decided to rest for a few days before continuing with his journey. He moved about from household to household, talking with the people, exchanging gossip, and accepting what hospitality was offered to him, for the people were very friendly and unused to seeing travelers from foreign parts. At one small house he came upon an old man making ready for a journey.

"Where are you going?" asked the young man, and the old man explained that he wished to see a wise and learned king in another land. He had heard of the king's generosity and compassion and wanted to see the great man for himself. The two men talked for a while and then sat down to eat together. Only a meager meal was placed on the table, and Dorje now used to having whatever food he desired, took the golden bowl from his chuba and ordered it to fill with meat. The old man looked on in amazement as the bowl complied with the young man's wishes.

"That is a magic bowl," the old man exclaimed, "where did you get it?" The young man related the story of the demons and his terrifying experience of a few nights past. The old man listened, then said, "A bowl such as that would be very useful to me on my journey. I would not have to carry food. Will you sell it to me?" The young man laughed, "This bowl is too precious to sell." Hurriedly he replaced it in his chuba.

The old man, his eyes twinkling, left the room and returned with an old wooden staff. Handing it to the young man he said, "This is a magic staff. Just ask it to fetch something for you." Dorje took the staff, it was old and notched, but felt smooth to the touch. Looking around the room he picked out a fur-trimmed hat lying on the floor near the old man's traveling bags. "Fetch the hat," the young man ordered the staff, and straight away the staff flew from his grasp, returning seconds later with the hat.

"This would indeed be a very useful staff," Dorje said, and taking the golden bowl from his ambac he agreed to exchange it for the magic staff. The two men said their farewells and the young man began his journey once again.

Before he had gone very far Dorje stopped. He turned to look in the direction of the old man's house, and holding the staff aloft he ordered it to fetch the golden bowl. The staff returned to the old man's house, beat him three times over the head and returned to Dorje with the golden bowl.

"Ah ha!," said the young man, "you have done as ordered, you will prove very useful, magic staff." And so saying he replaced the golden bowl in his chuba, took the staff in his right hand and walked away, as fast as possible, just in case the old man should follow and try to retrieve the magic object.

"Tashi delek," a voice shouted in greeting as Dorje was crossing a small river. He looked up, and sitting on the opposite bank was a shriveled old hermit. "Tashi delek," the young man replied and made his way to where the aged man was sitting. The old hermit's face creased with a smile, "Where are you heading?" he asked. Dorje replied that he was wandering about the country with no particular aim in mind, to which the old hermit chuckled and patted the ground beside him, beckoning the young man to sit.

The young man sat down beside the old hermit. Dorje noticed that his clothes were very ragged and torn, betraying the many years that the old man must have been homeless and destitute. "What do you do, old man?" he asked. "Oh, I sit here on the edge of the river watching the constant movement of the water," said the hermit. "Or, I wander about the valley just contemplating life." He smiled to himself, as if secretly enjoying a personal joke. "Sometimes," he continued, "I hammer prayers into the stones in exchange for alms; we get many pilgrims passing this way." The old hermit's hands fumbled beneath his worn robe and produced a beautifully carved "mani stone." "Would you like one?" he asked the young man.

"I am not traveling on pilgrimage," the young man replied, "and do not plan to visit any of the holy places." The old hermit replaced the stone, but as he did so Dorje caught site of a beautiful hammer hidden in the folds of the old man's garment. "Is that the hammer you use to carve the prayers into the stones?" he asked. The old man gave him a quick glance and

117

covered the hammer. "No," he replied, "not that hammer, it is too precious."

Dorje's curiosity was aroused, and he questioned the old hermit relentlessly. "Why is it precious?" he asked. "Do tell me." At last the old man gave in to his questioning. "With this hammer I can build houses of iron," he said. "Then why do you not use it?" asked the young man. The old hermit gave him a long searching look. "What use have I for an empty house?" he said. "I am happy being homeless." "But you can build houses for others," Dorje continued, "and be very rich."

The hermit folded his hands in his lap, gazed into the distance, and said, "I look for riches that money cannot buy; I seek the treasure that is hidden in my being. If I build houses for people, even though I ask no reward, I will be bringing only envy and dissatisfaction upon others, for there will always be someone wanting a house; there would be no end to the demands."

"Give the hammer to me," said Dorje, "for I can make better use of it than you." The old hermit shook his head, but did not speak. "I will give you something in exchange," Dorje continued, and taking the golden bowl from his chuba he proceeded to show the old man how it produced food and drink.

Slowly, the hermit reached into the folds of his robe and brought out the hammer. Handing it to the young man he said, "Take it. I will have the bowl; it will be far more useful to me than the hammer that makes iron houses." Dorje handed over the bowl, stood up, bade the old hermit goodbye, and went on his way.

Before he had walked very far, Dorje once again sent the staff to fetch back the golden bowl. Then, having three magic objects in his possession, he happily continued his journey.

For many a day he wandered, enjoying his freedom and feeling full of happiness. When he wanted a meal he asked his golden bowl, when he wished for shelter and rest he built an iron house, and when he wanted to relax and entertain himself he sent his magic staff to fetch things. Sometimes, if something he desired belonged to another traveler he met on the way, he would just send his staff to fetch it. He did not look upon it as stealing—just making use of the wonderful luck that had been bestowed upon him.

"I am indeed a fortunate man," he thought, and with a long contented sigh he let his hand drop to his side, feeling for his amulet. It was gone! Despite the fact that he had the three magic objects, he felt a shiver of foreboding run through his body as he realized he was without the protection of his amulet.

One day, Dorje came upon a withered old lady, standing outside a small hut on the edge of a gently sloping hill. The old lady was busy with a pair of black leather bellows, puffing at the air. The young man approached her. "Are you trying to set fire to the air, old lady?" he laughed, only to be met with her cold gaze as she turned to face him. Then, furiously, she began beating at the air with the bellows again.

Within seconds rain began to fall. . . .

Suddenly, the sky that had hitherto been clear and bright, clouded over. A darkness came over the land and a loud clap of thunder shook the ground on which they stood. Within seconds rain began to fall, and was soon torrenting down;

119

raindrops the size of small ponds dropped all around them. Dorje was soaked to the skin, and was swept off his feet by the heavy rain. The old lady shrieked with delight, laughed and danced around, waving the bellows above her head.

Dorje took out his hammer and beat it three times on the ground. Immediately a nine-storied iron house sprang up from nowhere, enclosing and sheltering the young man and the old lady within its walls. The old lady cried out in amazement and backed away from Dorje who was standing in a corner, laughing. "How did you work such magic?" she cried. "Tell me, what power do you possess?" The young man just waved his hammer in the air and carried on laughing; he was amused by the old lady's look of complete astonishment. The old lady left the house and returned minutes later with another pair of bellows. "The black bellows," she said, "bring rain for eighteen days. These white bellows bring sunshine. Tell me how you do your magic and I will give you the bellows." Dorje declined to tell the old lady that it was the hammer that built the house, and still chuckling, he waved goodbye and was gone.

When he had reached the bottom of the hill he sent the staff to fetch the two pairs of bellows, which it did, and then the happy young man began to walk toward the next village.

While sleeping that night, Dorje had disturbed dreams. Thoughts of his homeland invaded his sleeping and when he awoke he was full of longing to return. "With my magic objects," he thought, "no one, not even the king will be able to dispute my power." So, he began the long journey to back to the land of Ndu.

After many weeks Dorje arrived home. When he reached his mother's house it was far into the night. He woke his mother, and despite her protests, took her to the gates of the king's palace. Banging his hammer on the ground three times, he built a nine-storied house of iron, and taking his mother inside he barred and bolted the doors against intrusion.

Next morning, all of the kingdom gathered to look at the house which had suddenly sprung up over night. There was much speculation, and many of the men took the opportunity to gamble by placing bets as to how the house came to be there. Then, one of the people saw Dorje's face at the window. "The disrespectful son has returned," the voice rose above the crowd and brought silence on the gathering. "He who brought trouble on us by his foolish ways," the voice continued, "it is he who has built the house. Quickly, go tell the king."

The king, who was already angered by having an iron house placed right next to the palace, was even more enraged to find that it was the exiled young man esconced therein. He ordered all of the men of the kingdom to assemble outside the house; each has to bring a bucket of fuel and a pair of bellows. Then, with the yak-chips, logs, and coal piled around the base of the house, the men lit the fuel and then went to work with their bellows, fanning the small flames until they became an inferno. The iron house began to melt, slowly, as the flames reached an intense heat that made the metal white-hot at the base of the nine-storied house.

Dorje ran to the top story of the house, and leaning out of one of the windows, began to fan the air with his pair of black bellows. Rain fell, sending the people running for shelter, and damping the fire within seconds. The king was more angry than he had ever been. He sent his guards to watch over the house and prevent the son or his mother from leaving. "I will starve them to death," he cried, "I will be rid of this man for good."

But, what the king did not know, of course, was that the young man had his golden bowl which produced all the food and drink he and his mother needed. Many days passed, and the king began to despair. He sent a messenger to see the young man and declare a truce. "Bring him to me," the king ordered, "tell him I will not harm him."

So, Dorje went to see the king, and peace was made between them. The young man became very popular in the kingdom, as with his magic objects he helped all the people. When they needed rain to grow the crops, he gave them rain; when they needed sunshine to ripen the crops, he gave them sunshine. To the poor he gave food, and his staff was used to fetch and carry things for the infirm and old people of the kingdom.

The king became very jealous of the young man's power, for the people gave him more honor than they afforded their own king. Determined to be rid of the young man, the king began to ask questions as to how the young man came to possess the magic objects. Dorje had not been wise with his tongue, and had told several people about his night on the tree when he met the fearful demons. When the king heard this, he decided on a plan to bring the young man to grief. Sending one of his old servants to borrow the staff, the king sent it on a strange mission.

"Staff, bring to me the king of the demons," he said. The staff flew into the air, and was gone for many hours. It returned in the dead of night, and following behind, in all his fearful glory, was the king of the demons. The king was terrified at meeting with such an ugly, vicious being, but summoning up all his courage he explained to the king of the demons why he had sent for him.

"In the iron house," he said, "dwells a man who is the possessor of a magic bowl, the bowl he stole from a demon." The king of the demons, blood dribbling from his mouth, and his bloodshot eyes gleaming with untold horror, disappeared in a flash. It was the last the king saw of him, but next day the people of the kingdom found the young man dead, his heart torn out, and his magic objects gone. All except one, for the king was now the owner of the magic staff, which he used to restore his power in the kingdom.

THE MAGIC BAMBOO

THE SHUTTLECOCK ROSE HIGH in the air to the sound of delighted laughter. As it descended, the young girl, her waist-length black hair flowing about her head as she twisted and leapt, deftly kicked the little copper ball of the shuttlecock with the side of her foot to her sister, shouting her score on having kept the shuttlecock in the air. The three sisters' movements were like an improvised, graceful dance, as they leapt, ran, and kicked to keep the shuttlecock aloft.

Nyima, the youngest, gave a despairing yell, realizing that she had kicked the shuttlecock toward the dense bamboo grove. Her two sisters joined Nyima as she struggled to part the bamboos in an effort to find the shuttlecock. The middle sister, Yulma, sat on the grass for a few minutes to recover her breath.

"Listen," she said to her sisters, "I think father has come back." She stood up and ran toward the house, disappearing through the archway leading into the courtyard, calling "Pa-la, Pa-la!" The other two sisters almost reluctantly began to move toward the archway, but Yulma was already coming back toward them. "It was only the wind banging the door," she called.

Nyima, the youngest of the three, looked at her elder sister. "I still can't get used to the house like this." "I know," Dolma replied, "Nor can I." She stopped to pick some meadow foxtail, looping the stalk around itself and "firing the bud," seeing how far it would go. "The house is so empty, so lifeless," she said.

The three sisters' movements were like an improvised, graceful dance, as they kicked the shuttlecock.

Nyima sat down on the grass and watched Dolma, as Yulma joined them. The three beautiful girls were each lost in their own memories, their own loss, as they each thought of their mother. "It was always so alive," Nyima murmured. "The kitchen busy," Yulma said, "Something always seemed to be cooking." "So many visitors," Dolma fired the foxtail, "it was unusual if someone was not staying." "The teapot," Nyima said, "Do you remember? The teapot was always on the brazier, night and day. There was always someone needing help."

Nyima took a new shuttlecock out of her ambac, the pocket formed by the fold of her gown over her chest, and slowly, thoughtfully brushed her face with the feathers. "I miss her stories," Yulma said. "I think every child n the village heard her stories at one time or another." "Pa-la used to bring home friends, other merchants," Dolma said. "Yes, life was very different." "We are very lucky to be touched by a life like Ama-la," said Yulma. Their grief was still a raw wound and it bled easily.

In silence they thought of their mother. Nyima wiped her eyes with the long sleeve of her blouse—from a distance they

124

could just hear the rhythmic cheerful song of the women win-
nowing corn. The voice of the muezzin was carried by the breeze
as he called the Moslem faithful to pray at the small town's
ancient mosque. His long chant had a poignancy about it, a
quality that touched the depths of the heart, and the young
girls, glancing at each other, saw that they all had tears silently
coursing down their cheeks.

Their laughter at each other's attempts to hide their tears
broke the tension, and tears mingled with laughter. Yulma sat
beside Dolma and they fought one another with meadow fox-
tails, laughing and shouting when one succeeded in hitting the
other.

Nyima tossed the shuttlecock into the air and practiced
kicking it, with all the grace for which she was known. Lithe and
agile, she danced with the shuttlecock. She had moved quite a
few yards away from her sisters, toward the bamboo grove,
when a misjudged kick sent the shuttlecock spinning and wheel-
ing high into the bamboos.

"Kunjosum," Nyima cried out, "I will never find it now."
She looked despairingly at the grove. The bamboo was her
father's special pride, and worth a great deal. The legends her
mother had told about it, for the grove was very ancient, came
to Nyima's mind. She remembered seeing the massive bamboo
trees in the very center of the grove, the ones that were over ten
feet across and a hundred feet high and that blossomed only
when they were a hundred and thirty years old, or more. The
trees at the edge of the grove were saplings and their oval leaves,
like plates held up to the sun, did not cast deep shadows, but
still Nyima felt very nervous as she began to search for the
shuttlecock. Vigorously she began to sing to herself, the crush-
ing and breaking of twigs and stalks accompanying her as she
parted the undergrowth. She had the uncomfortable feeling of
being watched, and though fully aware of how silly it was, every
few minutes she looked round, unable to bear the suspense.
Nothing was there except the birds: startled by her sudden
movement they flew through the trees, twittering angrily.

125

Weary from searching the ground, Nyima slowly stood up and stretched herself. It occurred to her that the shuttlecock might have been caught in the leaves of the bamboo trees. She looked up at them—they seemed to jostle one another for space, so closely did the bamboo grow. She could hear the laughter of her two sisters in the distance, mingled with the sound of insects busy in the undergrowth, and the calls of birds as they darted about in the bamboo trees. "It is beautiful," she thought, and yet she had a feeling of apprehension. Nyima wanted to leave the grove, but she continued searching.

The sounds of cracking twigs and rustling grass chilled Nyima with fear. Now she knew that someone was in the grove. She longed to run, but had to stay, she had to know what was in the grove. The rustling and the movement among the bamboos grew more recognizable . . . footsteps . . . Nyima stopped herself from running, but as quickly as she could without arousing the suspicions of the intruder, she left the grove and then ran to her sisters.

"Quickly, someone is in the bamboo grove, what shall we do?"

"Are you sure!" Dolma stood up and started walking toward the grove.

"Dolma, wouldn't it be better," Nyima said nervously, "to lock ourselves in the house? We have no protection." But Dolma was walking firmly toward the bamboo grove with Yulma beside her. Yulma signalled for her sister to be quiet when they reached the edge of the grove, and for Dolma to listen

"I can't hear anything," she said after a few minutes, then "Wait! Yes, now I can hear, someone *is* in there!"

"They're trying to steal our bamboo," Nyima said angrily. "What are we going to do?" "Pa-la gave us strict instructions not to let anyone take the bamboo!" said Dolma.

"The sword!" cried Nyima, and ran as fast as she could toward the house. Her two sisters felt her absence weigh very heavily; they looked silently at each other, both aware of unspoken fears as they heard the intruder moving closer through the bamboo grove.

"Here she comes." Yulma sounded relieved as she and Dolma watched Nyima running toward them with a heavy sword, four feet long, the hilt bound in silver and decorated with large lumps of coral, and the scabbard covered in sharkskin and studded with turquoise and coral. When she reached them, Nyima immediately tried to unsheath the sword, but it refused to be moved from the scabbard.

"Oh, no, sword! Please, please do come out," Nyima moaned, while her sisters tried to help.

"How did it get like this?" Nyima asked, pulling hard at the sword, for she could see now that the scabbard was slightly bent.

"I think I remember," Yulma said. "Pa-la and a merchant had an argument; it came to a fight. Pa-la hit the merchant with the sword still in the scabbard! Ama-la managed to save the merchant, but he ended up with a split skull." It took the combined efforts of all three girls before the scabbard reluctantly gave up the sword.

Nyima walked closer to the bamboo grove, her sister's anxiety increasing as they watched. She tried to look fierce and, holding the sword firmly in both hands, walked nearer to the grove, a look of grim determination on her face. Nyima stopped and then they all heard a loud cracking of breaking saplings as someone moved through the bamboos. They heard a knife slashing, then saw bamboo trees toppling out of sight as the intruder cut them down. The girls stood close to one another; now they were really frightened.

"Come out," Nyima shouted firmly. "Come out now!" She glanced at her sisters apprehensively as she saw the form of a man emerge from the shadow of the trees.

As one, the three girls backed away as he walked out of the shadows and into the sunshine. Nyima moved the sword up and down in what she hoped was a threatening gesture. The sun caught the young man's perfectly set teeth as he stood quite relaxed, casually holding a dagger and laughing at Nyima's attempts to look fierce.

127

"Don't you dare laugh!" Dolma said pugnaciously, and stood beside her sister, fists clenched. Any confidence Nyima felt in the threat she presented with the sword evaporated, and she shifted her feet uneasily. The young man growled, and suddenly lunged at Nyima with his dagger. She cried out, lost her footing, and he knocked the sword aside as though it were a stick. Dolma and Yulma launched themselves in a fury at the young man, pounding, kicking, and biting. Laughing, and yelling with pain, the young man fended them off, while Nyima danced round the flailing group, shouting to her sisters to keep still so that she could get at him with the sword. Eventually he held the two struggling girls firmly by the hair.

"Let them go," Nyima hissed through gritted teeth, and advanced with the sword. Easily the young man moved his dagger, so that it was only a fraction of an inch from Yulma's throat.

"Now behave yourself, and put that sword down."

Nyima was furious, both at the young man's intrusion into their life, and at his patronizing attitude toward their attempts to guard the family home. Yulma and Dolma were cursing the intruder as they struggled to free themselves. The young man let them go, and for the first time the girls really saw him properly. He was well built, with a lean, deeply tanned face, an aquiline nose, and the three girls quickly saw the charm of his laughing eyes and infectious smile. He wore a sheepskin-lined chuba, leaving one arm and his chest was bare, and from his brisk, graceful movements the girls recognized a nomad, or more likely, one of the brigands who regularly attacked the caravans.

"What are you doing here?" Dolma inquired.

"Just looking," replied the handsome stranger.

"Don't lie!" Dolma snapped, "You were stealing our bamboo."

The young man laughed, but did not answer, gently running the edge of his dagger against his chin. He so obviously assessed the three girls that they each blushed, as he slowly walked around the garden and looked over the house.

"You should go now," Dolma said, "Our father will be back soon." The young man stopped, looked at the girls, and said, "I should like to meet the man who has three such beautiful daughters, and such a fine bamboo grove."

Dolma felt she had not convinced the man of her father's impending return.

"It is better that you do not see our father," Dolma continued, "and you have still not told us what brought you here."

The young man shrugged and chuckled, "You are so suspicious."

"We have good reason to be," Dolma replied. "What *did* bring you here?"

The young man smiled at her, "Your beguiling laughter." He took a small round polished wooden snuff box from his ambac, tapped some of the powdered tobacco onto his thumbnail and inhaled it. The sisters looked at one another, their eyes wide, at a loss as to what their next move should be. Dolma, who thought that there was more to the man than met the eye, and feeling uncertain that he was just a common thief, said "Come inside and have some tea."

"You are mad," Yulma murmured to Nyima and Dolma, fixed the man with an icy stare, and then marched toward the house, with the others following quickly in her footsteps.

Over tea the young man talked a little about himself, and soon the girls were competing with each other, though it was cloaked in a suitable expression of shyness, for the young man's attention as they drank their tea in one of the best rooms in the house. The room's supporting pillars had carved wooden capitals, and finely woven rugs covered the divans. A beautiful shrine was the center-piece of the room, with fruit piled high onto its silver offering dishes. The twenty silver butter lamps on the shrine also illuminated the room, which had only small rice-paper-covered windows set high in the wall.

"Have you traveled from far?" Nyima asked.

"From U-Tsang," he replied.

"Tell us your history," Dolma asked, thinking that this young man must have some interesting stories to tell.

He smiled, thought for a moment, and looked at the girls with such obvious frankness that they all blushed again. While he considered, the young man lifted the jade teacup from its silver stand. Although he took only a sip, as soon as he lowered the cup, Nyima filled it again from a large copper and brass teapot with the handle and spout finely wrought in the form of a dragon. The young man fingered his large rough turquoise earring, so heavy on its gold hoop that it needed a leather thong over his ear to keep it from tearing his earlobe.

"First," the young man said, "I want to hear about you." He smiled at them again, with a slightly quizzical look on his face. "Why are you here alone?"

"Our father is at the market in Batang," Dolma replied, "and our mother died a few months ago. The servants have all gone," but her words faded as Yulma cast her a worried look. "Our father is expected back from the market very soon," she continued.

The young man smiled, and she was aware of his slightly mocking tone as he muttered "Yes," fully aware that she was making feeble attempts to cover up the fact that they had been left alone for some time.

"I shall look forward to meeting your father," the young man said. Involuntarily, the three girls gave a cry, and looked at one another. The young man took another sip of tea and ate one of the sweet breads that the girls had arranged so neatly on little silver dishes in front of him.

"We all think," Nyima said nervously "that it would be better if you do not meet our father. What I mean," she corrected herself, "is that you should not meet him like this. He will not like finding you here." She was sitting crosslegged on a rug-covered divan, plaiting her hair with colored thread, and the young man thought her quite attractive in her faintly defiant way.

"But you invited me here," he said, settling himself more comfortably on the divan, and taking off his red fox fur hat. Nyima noticed that he had close-cropped hair, like a monk.

Yulma did not look at the young man but spun the prayer wheel on the low carved table, a little bell recording each revolution. "Our father," she said, "does not like visitors coming to see us unless he has invited them himself, or has first approved of them." The young man thought that she had the most expressive eyes he had ever seen. They spoke their own story of sadness and loneliness.

"We do not have many visitors," Nyima added and watched the young man tap some snuff onto his thumbnail and inhale again. "Since our mother died," she continued, "our father has been a lonely man. He does not want to invite people home yet."

"You know," the young man replaced the top of the snuff flask and tucked it back in his ambac, "there are stories I heard at the inn that your father almost keeps you prisoners—that you see no one."

Dolma made irritated, dismissive noises.

"People in the village do not understand our father. Do we look like prisoners?"

"No," the young man smiled. Nyima felt that Dolma's picture of the situation was as false as what the young man heard in the village.

"Our father . . . " Nyima continued to methodically plait her hair. "Well . . . " she paused again. "It is true that he does not like us to meet people without him. I suppose we don't mix as much of some of the other people of the village."

The young man read from her frank and direct gaze the unspoken story of how closely their father guarded the girls' lives and friendships.

"You have traveled?" he asked.

"Oh, yes," Dolma replied. "When our mother was alive we went with her and our father to the festivals at Batang."

"And danced with the men."

Dolma lowered her eyes. "No. Our father has been very strict about our forming relationships with men."

Yulma got up and poured more tea for everyone, carefully replacing the engraved silver lids on the cups.

"You have not told us your name," she said quickly, pouring the young man tea and offering him some biscuits.

"Tsering Wangdi."

"I am Yulma, and this is my eldest sister, Dolma, and my younger sister, Nyima." Yulma replaced the teapot on the brazier. Nyima felt irritated that this stranger, this intruder, should somehow make the sisters feel at such a disadvantage.

"Tsering, you must understand that our father is anxious for our future. He is looking for a suitable husband for us, who can be adopted into our family. When Pa-la dies he would become head of the family so that our inheritance will not be divided."

"Is that what you all want?" Tsering looked at the sisters, who were perplexed at the question.

"But why shouldn't we?" Yulma asked. "Look at what we have here. We have a beautiful home. Everything we could want." She smiled shyly at Tsering, her head slightly lowered.

"You have a beautiful home," Tsering agreed, looking 'round the room.

"Our estate," Nyima said quickly, "is the largest in the valley, so what need have we to go anywhere else?"

Tsering was looking out the window across the wide, beautiful valley. He smiled at Nyima. "Let me tell you something of myself. Many years ago I was a hermit. I was walled up in a cave and could only see a small patch of sky through a special hole in the roof. A trap door was built in the entrance to the cave so that food and water could be passed to me. For months I saw no one, as I thought about the meaning of life." Tsering paused and took a long drink of tea. "You know that we have had many famous hermits who have become enlightened and then brought great blessings to many people, but this was not to be my way." He paused and then pointed at the teapot.

"You all see the dragon decoration on the teapot? The design of the pillars, the foliage worked into the decoration of the brazier? Everywhere in the room there are intricate decorations and designs, and all of them from the teapot to the shrine are symbols of ultimate truth. But they are not the truth itself." Tsering reached over and touched the knob of the teapot lid. "What is this, Dolma?"

"A teapot," she said automatically, then joined in her sisters' laughter as she saw her mistake. "A lotus."

Dolma frowned with concentration. Nyima had finished the lengthy job of plaiting her hair and was fixing red tassels to the end of the braid.

"Well, a lotus means enlightenment," Dolma said. "The Buddha sits on a lotus throne."

"There is more," Tsering said.

"Surely it symbolizes," Yulma replied for her sister, "Man's spiritual strugle. We are in the mud, in the earth, and through the murky waters the lotus climbs to blossom in the clear pure air above."

"Exactly," Tsering said forcefully, "and that was the lesson I had to learn. I was not meant to be a hermit; it cut me off from the world, and I realized the mistake I was making. I had to be in the world. Like the lotus, rooted in the world . . . . "

"And now," Nyima interrupted, "you are growing through the murky waters of life to emerge into the pure heavens as a blossom of enlightenment?" She sounded disbelieving. Tsering laughed.

"I am far too ignorant to think of such things; I still have to learn how to begin the journey. But I have learned the difference between the symbol and the reality."

"What do you mean?" Nyima again had the aggressive, challenging note in her voice.

"Do you not see that your life here is like a symbol, or a reflection of the real world? You are not living in the real world."

Nyima laughed. "You are are foolish now. Of course we are. We are here with you; is that not real?"

"What do you know of life outside your estate?"

"We have been told by Pa-la . . . " Tsering smiled at Nyima's admission.

"The world is a far more beautiful place than you could ever imagine," Tsering said, "but it is also far more terrible than you could imagine." He laughed. "Far more frightening than finding me in your bamboo grove!"

"I can believe it," Nyima said, "if you have anything to do with it!"

"It is the world," Tsering continued, "of good and evil, of pain and joy. But it is the world in which we live. If I shut the lotus flower up in a box it would not grow. I was shut up in a hermitage. You are as much shut away here."

Nyima laughed, clearly not believing him.

"The lotus grows healthy and strong because it is rooted in the world, using everything to feed and sustain it." He looked at Nyima. "You have much to learn."

Nyima reached out and touched his hand, and before Tsering realized it she had removed one of his large rings.

"Well, Tsering, let us talk and see how much you have to teach me." As he reached across to grab hold of her hand she darted out of the room. He followed quickly after her.

Later, when Nyima and Tsering returned, the young girl murmured softly to Yulma, "I am sure I do not understand him. See if you can understand what he wants." She smiled and slipped the ring into her hand. Yulma giggled.

It was sometime later that Yulma and Tsering returned to the room. Yulma went over to Dolma. "You are the oldest Dolma. Perhaps you will understand what Tsering is trying to teach us." Yulma's eyes were full of laughter as she dropped Tsering's ring into her sister's hand. "Surely this time," Dolma said to the young man, "you will be able to re-claim your ring?" He smiled.

"Really Tsering, we think you ought to go now." Nyima undid the small leather pouch at her belt and took out some tinder. Holding a few strands of dried grass mixed with soot together with the fint in her left hand, she struck the stone sharply with the curved metal steel blade that formed the bottom of the pouch. After a few abortive sparks, the tinder caught fire and Nyima held the flame to a mustard-oil lamp on a slate shelf set in the wall. "It is close to dusk," she continued "and Pa-la will certainly return by the time the sun goes down."

As she spoke Nyima carefully lit the other mustard-oil lamps in the room.

"Come on Tsering!" Dolma tossed his red fox fur hat at him. Tsering left it where it lay on the divan beside him and tapped out some snuff.

"As I said, I am looking forward to meeting your father."

"No, please Tsering." Yulma got up and stood in front of him; "Please go for our sakes." She looked at him with large expressive eyes, but he only returned her gaze with a slightly mocking glance.

"Why are you so interested in meeting our father?" Dolma asked as she fed more yak chips onto the brazier, and the room became full of a throat-scorching blue haze.

"Many in the village talk not only of your father's three beautiful daughters, but of the treasure he has hidden." Tsering began coughing from the reeking brazier smoke and blew the snuff from his thumbnail.

"No," Dolma said forcefully, "it is not true."

Yulma looked at Tsering sadly. "So you have just come to steal?"

He walked over to her and stroked her hair, smiling. "Do you not want to give me a parting gift?"

Nyima shouted at him. "You are a thief, a brigand. You have taken our hospitality and cheated us!"

Tsering laughed. "Of what have I cheated you? I did not ask for anything, did I? I did not ask for your hospitality." As he spoke Tsering walked round the room, tapping the pillars with the hilt of his knife. Nyima could see a certain truth in what he said.

"What are you doing?" she asked.

"Many people store their treasure in hollow pillars." Tsering smiled broadly at them.

"There is not any gold," Dolma insisted. "Tsering, please listen," the girl took hold of his arm, "there really is not any gold concealed in the pillars."

Tsering gave her a disbelieving look, and walked over to the corner of the room where he began tapping the wall of

135

tamped earth which had set like concrete in the dry cold climate.

Nyima went over to a large brass coffer decorated with coral. "Dolma," she whispered, and held her hand out. The eldest sister followed Nyima's eyes to the coffer, then produced a large key and gave it to her youngest sister. Nyima opened the coffer. "Tsering!" The young man looked up and walked over to her. He looked in the coffer, it was full of silver coins. "Take these, Tsering," Nyima said, "and be on your way."

"Do you have any saddle bags?" "Yes," Yulma said, and left the room, returning after a few minutes with brilliantly colored, woven saddle bags. Tsering filled the bags with the silver coins. He slung the saddle bags over his shoulder and turned to look at Nyima. She stiffened at his faintly mocking smile. "Tsering, now please go."

The young man laughed. "You must think I am a very simple man?"

"No," Nyima interrupted, "we have given you all the money in the house, please Tsering, you have nothing to lose, please." She smiled up at him and gently tweaked his ear, "Go, you have got all that you came for."

The young man sat on the divan and dropped the heavy saddle bags onto the floor beside him. "Nyima, Nyima," he chided, "the more you have insisted that I go, the longer I have stayed, and the richer I have become!" He tried to kiss Yulma, who angrily evaded him. "Do not play with me," Tsering continued, "you know as well as I do that your father has treasure hidden in the house—he must have." Yulma took Tsering's hand in hers saying, "You have taken much from us today, do you want to leave us without any inheritance?"

Tsering chuckled, "There is enough for all of us, and any deficiency will soon be made up." He chucked Yulma under the chin, and sat back on the divan looking at the three girls in turn.

"Listen," Nyima said, "I have an idea. If I give you a token that you can redeem, we will give you whatever treasure we have when we next see you."

Tsering thought for a moment. "Very well," he said, and got up.

Nyima took one of the red tassels from her hair, and tied it around a foot-long piece of bamboo. "If, whenever you meet us, you show this token to redeem our pledge, we give you whatever we are able to give. My sisters and I will abide by the pledge." Nyima looked at Yulma. "I agree, Tsering," Yulma replied. The young man looked at Dolma. "Very well," Dolma said sadly. "I agree."

"Well, three beautiful sisters," Tsering picked up the saddle bags, "Farewell!"

The fat man had been totally absorbed in mah jong for the past ten hours. Tired and tense, he continually brushed his tiny moustache with his fingers. Like all Tibetans, he had very little body hair, and so was particularly proud of his moustache. It had been carefully and assiduously cultivated, and painfully shaped with tweezers. His companions joked with him, saying his moustache resembled a milk-pail hook.

The fat man was well-dressed, and had the insignia of a government official and noble. He was wearing a fine green satin chuba, a large pendant turquoise earring in one ear, and a button turquoise earring in the other. His pigtail was wound round his head, and plaited into the hair was a large turquoise and silver amulet box, worn on the crown of his head. His companion appeared to have lost all interest in the game, as he looked down from the flat roof of the inn towards the narrow wooden bridge across which rode Dolma, Yulma, and Nyima.

"It is true what they say about Jigme Wangchuk's daughters; they are the most beautiful girls in the district," he said to the noble without looking around. "The men who become their husbands will indeed be lucky men."

The three sisters were dressed in their finest festival clothes, and were arrayed in all their richest jewelry, their hair built up and extensively decorated with embossed silver plaques studded with coral and turquoise. Both ends of the bridge were crowded with boisterous and admiring young men.

The nobleman's temper faded, as he saw that his companion's comments were indeed correct; the three sisters were exceptionally striking women.

A few moments after the girls left the bridge, the noble saw a young man in the crowd trying to attract their attention with a decorated bamboo stick. The bamboo, the fat man saw, achieved a remarkable effect, for when the girls saw it they immediately began to divest themselves of their jewelry. One unclipped a large amber, a turquoise, and a decorated silver amulet box that hung across her breast and gave them to the young man. Another gave him her beautiful earrings, and the third, her richly encrusted belt. The girls waved at the young man as they rode on, urging their horses to catch up with their father, who was oblivious to what had happened, so engrossed was he in conversation with a riding companion.

The fat man was intrigued; what magic power did the bamboo stick possess, that it could bring its owner such riches?

Tsering stored his treasure in the bag inside his chuba and went into a tavern to buy his friends some chang.

"Jigme, it's your turn." But the fat man's thoughts were no longer on mah jong. "Jigme, did you hear me?" To his companion's surprise the fat man replied by throwing in his hand and then, grunting from the exertion, rising to his feet.

Tsering, feeling a hand on his shoulder, looked up.

"I would like to speak with you privately," the fat man said, having to shout close to Tsering's ear to make himself heard above the din. The young man was puzzled, but interested. Telling his friends he would be back shortly, he picked up his wooden tankard of barley beer and followed the fat man into a private room. When they had sat down on a divan, a serving girl gave them fresh chang.

"My friend," the nobleman's words were so heavy with guile that Tsering's suspicion increased, "I have seen you around the market, and my friends have told me something about you."

Tsering, looking very young and unsophisticated in comparison to the suave and polished nobleman, listened attentively, obviously, the nobleman was glad to note, conscious of the honor being done to him.

"You have come from the Chang Thang plains?"

"Yes, Honorable Sir," Tsering answered, with a slightly deferential inclination of the head.

"It is said that you are now quite a rich man, from the money you have made by winning horse races."

Tsering laughed. "The gods have been kind to me."

The fat man thoughtfully sucked the barley beer through a straw. "You have your own horse?" he asked.

"No," Tsering replied, "I have been riding a friend's."

The fat man grunted, as slowly and with difficulty he got up. "Come with me, Tsering." The fat man led Tsering down a dark corridor, through an outer door into the courtyard of the inn. He spoke to one of his servants, who went to the stables surrounding the courtyard, and in a few minutes came out leading a beautiful silver-grey horse.

As a nomad, Tsering had been born in the saddle, but he had no doubt in his own mind that this was the finest horse he had ever seen, even its color marked it out as a "blue" horse, rarely seen in a lifetime. Children playing in the courtyard crowded as close as they respectfully could to the two men and the "magic blue horse."

The fat man smiled at Tsering's reaction. "I see you like my horse."

"Like him! Honored Sir, it is a privilege to be in the presence of such a horse."

"Try him," the noble said, indicating that Tsering should mount the horse. With an ease born of a lifetime with horses, Tsering slid onto the horse's bare back. The noble handed him the reins, and Tsering urged the horse into a trot out of the courtyard. The children ran in the wake of the horse and at the gates to the inn watched Tsering put the horse through its paces. The fat man took a little snuff, and smiled to himself at Tsering's exultant cry as he sped by.

"A horse of the gods!" Tsering said to the fat man as he dismounted in the courtyard. The two men watched the horse being led back to the stable by the servant, each waiting for the other to make the first move. In silence, Tsering followed the fat man back to their room. The noble ordered more chang for them both, then tipped some snuff from a snuff horn for Tsering and himself, saying, "You do not have a horse, and you would like to have this horse?" He spoke as though it was a suggestion Tsering had made to him. He thoughtfully inhaled the snuff. "And what could you give me for him?"

The young man coughed. "Such horses are not sold, unless for all the Dalai Lama's treasure. I am not the Dalai Lama."

"Occasionally in a man's life, the gods smile upon him, and each man, I believe, is given certain opportunities, but few are great enough to seize them," the noble said.

"You really mean to sell the blue horse?" Tsering sounded disbelieving.

"My friend," the noble said, "look at me. I used to be able to ride and do the blue horse justice, but now . . . well now it is all I can do to get on a horse," he looked Tsering squarely in the eyes. "The blue horse has been very good to me in the past. It was born to run like the wind, not to be just an adornment to my household. You could do justice to that horse."

Tsering was confused—was this man really suggesting that he should buy the precious horse? "I could never give you enough for it."

There was a long pause, and Tsering knew they had reached the moment when the fat man's real motives would be revealed.

"You are, I think, quite right. I doubt that even the fine jewelry you have with you would be of sufficient value to purchase the blue horse."

Tsering smiled to himself, now he began to see what the nobleman really sought.

"What interested me," the nobleman continued, "was the means by which you got the treasure."

"You mean the magic bamboo?" Tsering's use of the word "magic" awoke in the nobleman both excitement and caution.

"You joke with me," he said.

140

"You saw what happened when I pointed the bamboo at the three sisters," Tsering said, almost to himself. "Indeed, the gods blessed me when I received the magic bamboo. Already it has brought me much wealth." He laughed, "Not enough to buy a blue horse, but give me time." Tsering spoke as though closing the subject, and offered snuff from his flask to the fat man. The noble took the snuff, and frowning, grunted his thanks. Tsering could almost see him thinking out how to pursue the matter.

"You would like to have the horse?"

"Of course."

"And in time you think you could buy him from me?"

"I could try; the magic bamboo would see to that, but the blue horse is surely beyond price."

"You are right," the fat man continued, "however, I have an idea that may solve the problem. I will give you the horse for the magic bamboo!"

Tsering looked surprised, then doubtful; his prolonged pause was an agony for the nobleman, the uncertainty making the bamboo seem even more desirable.

"It is done," Tsering said at last, and handed over the piece of bamboo.

Later that afternoon Tsering was showing off his magnificent mount to an admiring crowd when four of the nobleman's servants rode up, and to his horror and surprise, seized Tsering and took him to the nobleman's house. The fat man was pacing the floor; as soon as Tsering was brought before him he began to hurl abuse and accusations at him. Tsering, with equal anger, demanded to know what had happened to cause him to be so unjustly treated.

The fat man said that he had tried out the magic bamboo, with no success! He had seen the abbot of the local monastery out riding, and had pointed the bamboo at him. The abbot had stopped, looked at him for a few moments, then burst out laughing and went on with his ride. Not only had the noble been bitterly disappointed at the bamboo's ineffectiveness, but his dignity had suffered considerably.

Tsering began to laugh loudly. "Of course the abbot would laugh," he said.

"Because I looked so ridiculous!" the fat man said, by now screaming in near hysterical tones. "You can have your magic bamboo, and I will have my horse back, and see you punished for your trickery!"

"You do not understand; that is why the abbot laughed," Tsering said. "If you point the bamboo at a poor man it will not make him rich! What can he give you? The abbot is not wealthy, of course the bamboo would not work; he has nothing to give you."

The noble realized it was quite true when he thought about it.

"The general is a very rich man. Tomorrow he will be parading his men outside the village. Try the magic bamboo then," Tsering said, "and to make it even more effective have a likeness of the general painted on the bamboo."

Somewhat ungraciously the nobleman agreed to do this, but warned Tsering of the dire consequences that would befall him if the bamboo did not "perform."

The following day, the nobleman rode with his retainers to the general's parade. The troops had spent many hours polishing their breastplates and helmets. Almost all of the townspeople had gathered to watch the parade. As an official, the nobleman was given a special seat in a tent reserved for dignitaries, and was served tea and food while he watched.

"Quickly! Quickly! My horse!" the nobleman shouted to a servant. He was certainly not going to point the bamboo at the general from the ground, it would not befit his rank and dignity. So a few minutes later, as the general rode across the parade ground toward the official's tent, the noble rode out to meet him, and the general raised his hand in acknowledgment of what he took to be a courteous gesture of greeting.

The general, who was a superstitious and easily angered man, saw with horror, as he rode toward the noble, that the fat man was pointing a decorated bamboo stick at him, painted with a likeness of his own face! Furious and frightened at what was clearly an attempt to curse him, the general drew his sword and struck down the unsuspecting nobleman.

The nobleman was dead. The three sisters had learned much. And the young man was wealthy, had the horse of the gods, and did not need to fear any man, for it had come to pass as he had planned.

<hr />

NOTE: At parties or festivals often a boy who likes a girl will take her belt or something similar, only promising to give it back if the girl will meet him that night. Nyima has turned the tables on Tsering by taking his ring.

THE MISSING TREASURE

AS THE SETTING SUN SANK beneath the glacier-tipped mountain peaks, they glowed red as the embers of a fire. From the flat roofs of the houses of Lhasa children flew brightly colored kites from strings sprinkled with powdered glass. The children bobbed and weaved around one another—the kites shadowing their movements—as they laughed excitedly and attempted to cut each other's kite strings. A little boy of about six sat beside his uncle, a monk dressed in maroon robes. They watched the boy's kite sail higher and higher in the sky. Caught and held by the wind, it was so high that it appeared not to be moving. Still watching the kite, the boy said,

"Tell me a story, uncle."

The monk chuckled.

"An ancient story, then."

"A father said to his son," the monk began, " 'I am going to die soon, my son. Take my gold to your house. It is yours, but remember that you should not trust anybody, not even your wife.' The father hoped that his son, Sonam, would remember his advice and that he would understand the ways of the world.

"Now Sonam had a very good friend whose name was Tamchu. As children they had their lessons together and in the evenings played foot-shuttlecock. Tamchu lived in the next village with his wife and two little boys.

144

"One day Sonam decided to go on a pilgrimage to the holy monastery and he thought to himself, 'When he was alive my father told me not to trust anybody.' But when he thought of his friend Tamchu he could not believe that these words were true about him. Not Tamchu. So he took his two bags of gold nuggets to his friend's house and asked him, 'Tamchu-la, please keep my gold safe for me while I am away. This is the gold my father gave me when he died.'

"Tamchu said, 'Oh yes. Oh yes. I will keep your gold very carefully and when you return from your pilgrimage it will be safe for you. You do not need to worry. We are good friends.'

"So," the monk continued the story, "a year passed and Sonam returned from his pilgrimage. He went to Tamchu's home and asked his friend, 'May I have my gold back, Tamchu?'

" 'Oh I am so sorry, Sonam. We are unlucky, so unlucky. The gold has turned to sand!' Tamchu looked at his friend in amazement as he told him of this remarkable happening. But Sonam did not seem surprised and, after a few moments of silence, said, 'That is all right Tamchu. Do not worry. You did your best to look after my gold.'

"The two men ate together, and it seemed that the loss of the gold was almost forgotten. Later in the day Sonam said to his friend, 'Tamchu, I would like to look after your sons for a few months, as I do not have a family of my own. I would like to give them good food and good clothes. We should be very happy together at my home.'

" 'That is a very good idea Sonam!' Tamchu thought to himself, 'Although he has lost his gold to me, he wants to look after my sons. Well,' he thought, 'he is a very kind person.' So he said, 'Certainly Sonam. Please take my sons for as long as you wish.'

"Sonam took the boys to his home and looked after them very well. He then bought two little monkeys and gave them the boy's names. During the following days Sonam trained the monkeys so that when he called 'Tendzin come here!' the older monkey would run over to him. When Sonam called 'Thupten,

145

come here!' the young monkey went over to him. The monkeys understood very well and learned quickly.

"When Tamchu came to see his sons, Sonam looked very sad as he greeted his friend. 'I am so sorry, Tamchu. We are very unlucky, so unlucky. Your sons have turned into monkeys.' Tamchu was very upset and called out his son's names. Straight away the two little monkeys appeared and ran over to him. They grabbed Tamchu's hands and danced about him like little children. Tamchu was distressed and asked his friend, 'Sonam what can we do? How can we turn monkeys back into my sons?'

"Sonam thought for a moment and then said to his friend, 'That is easy,' but he sounded sad at the impossibility of such a thing, 'we need a lot of gold.' 'How much gold will do?' Tamchu asked. 'About two bags of gold nuggets, at least!'

" 'As soon as possible,' Tamchu said, 'I will bring the bags of gold.' And he hurried off to his home. Later he came back and gave Sonam the gold. Sonam took it and told his friend to wait while he went upstairs. A few moments later he returned.

" 'Here you are Tamchu. I have changed the monkeys back into human beings, into your sons.'

"Tamchu was delighted to have his sons back, but he looked sheepishly at Sonam. The two friends could not help laughing at one another."

At the end of the story the monk himself burst out laughing as he saw that his nephew's kite string had been cut while the boy listened to the story. The two of them watched the kite float across Lhasa valley towards the golden rooftops of the Potala.

BEWARE OF HONEY OFFERED ON
A SHARP KNIFE.

THE ISLAND OF
BEAUTIFUL WOMEN

O NCE A SHIP FULL OF MERCHANTS set sail on the high seas in search of riches. The merchants would be away for many months, for they planned to visit many ports and fill the ship's hold with rare and beautiful things to trade when they returned to their home port. For many weeks the ship moved noiselessly through the water, slowly cutting its way through the calm sea. Then, as if a curtain had been drawn across the sun, the sky became dark and angry, and a strong wind began to batter the sea, causing mighty waves to heave and toss the small ship until it completely lost direction and was at the mercy of the elements.

The storm seemed to last for many days, but just how many the merchants could not tell. During the relative light of daytime and the inky blackness of night they struggled to keep the ship afloat on the surging waters of the ocean. Just as the merchants had given up hope of ever seeing land again, they sighted a small island. As pleased as they were to see the land, they could also see the jagged rocks that formed the shoreline, as though waiting for the small ship to batter itself helplessly against them, meaning certain death for the merchants. The merchants could not decide whether to try and guide the ship away from the island, only to be finally beaten by the ever-strengthening storm, or to try and land on the rocky shore. But their minds were made up for them: the ship moved relentlessly toward the island as if driven by some unseen force.

The merchants tried with all their skill and strength to guide the ship safely onto land, but, as they had feared, the waves and wind won the battle and they were forced to abandon the ship and try to reach safety in small wooden boats. Many of the men were thrown from their craft by the huge waves and lost their lives trying to reach the island. Those that reached the beach safely fell down to their knees in thankful prayer for having been spared their lives.

Once the merchants had recovered from their frightening ordeal they began to organize a search of the land, and parties of men were sent out to survey the island. The leader of the merchants, together with six of his men, stayed behind on the beach to erect living quarters and search for edible plants and fruit. Food was not in short supply, for they soon discovered that the island was rich in all kinds of vegetation. As darkness fell, all but one of the search parties had returned to the beach. The surveyors reported that they had not seen any signs of people on the island, but that it was small and populated with many kinds of animals and birds. When the last party had still not returned at daybreak, the leader grew worried, and was just about to organize a search for them when he heard noises in the distance. It was the lost party, and with them were several of the most beautiful women the men had ever seen.

When they came to the beach the leader asked where they had been and where they had found the women. The men replied that they had found a small village populated only by women, and that they were all extremely beautiful. The women invited the merchants to come and live with them, for they explained that since their menfolk had gone to sea many months before and had not returned, they feared that the men were lost forever.

The merchants were very happy to join the women, and each took one of the beautiful beings for his wife. For several months all was well with the merchants. They lived very happily, and many of the wives gave birth to healthy children. The merchants would not have minded if they never returned to their home port again, for life was indeed like paradise on the little island.

After some time, the leader of the merchants began to notice that some of his men were missing, and on inquiring about them received no satisfactory answer. He decided to leave the village and walk to the beach in order to try and solve the mystery by spending some time in quiet meditation. On reaching the beach, the leader of the merchants looked out to sea where he could still see the mangled wreckage of the ship, now just a skeleton, half sunk into the deep sand.

The horse had wings, and seemed to give off a pure white light.

Then a horse appeared in the sky. The horse had wings, and seemed to give off a pure white light. The merchant could hardly believe his eyes, but as he was about to run away the horse landed on the beach in front of him and spoke:

"You are the leader of the merchants?"

The leader noticed that his voice was musical, and that where the horse stood the sand turned to gold dust.

"Yes," replied the merchant, "I am the leader."

The horse went on to explain how the island was inhabited by fearful flesh-eating demons, who appeared as beautiful women during the day. He had heard of the merchants' fate and had come to help them escape.

The leader said that he was indeed worried about the loss of some of his men, but that he could not imagine that the lovely women could be responsible. He also wondered how the magic horse had learned of their plight, but thought that perhaps under the circumstances he had better not ask.

"I am very happy here," he told the horse. "My wife has just given birth to a baby boy, and at night she stays in my home. I do not think that she is a flesh-eating demon."

The horse told the merchant to stay awake at night and watch; then he flew into the air, scattering gold dust from his hooves.

The merchant was most troubled by the meeting and what the horse had said. He thought that the horse must indeed be special, perhaps even Chenrezik himself come to help them, and so he decided to stay awake that night and watch.

Just as the horse had said, his beautiful wife left the house in the early hours of the morning, and together with the other women he saw her change into a horrible, ugly demon. They carried away one of the merchants, but the leader did not wish to follow and watch whatever was to become of the poor man. Instead he returned to his bed, but sleep did not come easily that night, and he made up his mind to return to the beach the next day in hope of seeing the horse again.

At daybreak the leader of the merchants made his way to the beach and was pleased to see that the horse was already waiting for him. The merchant thought he was a beautiful horse, with wings of golden brown and skin that shone with all the richness of gold. The light emitted from the horse's body was pure and white, but like a mist, insubstantial, almost ethereal. The merchant told the horse about the events of the previous night, and asked for help in getting off the island.

"We cannot repair the ship," he told the horse, "and the small boats that we have will not be able to survive in a storm."

The horse listened to the merchant, and then said, "If you and the rest of your men meet me on the beach I will carry you to safety, but it must be at the full moon, for the demons' power is not so great then."

The merchant agreed to meet the horse when the day of the next full moon arrived, and then bade the horse farewell until then.

"Do not worry," said the horse as he flew into the air, "I will be watching over you."

The merchant returned to the village to tell his men about the demons and to plan the escape. A meeting was held, at which only the men were allowed; when the leader told them of what he had seen, and about the magic horse, the men were all afraid. A plan was decided upon to save them all from perishing at the hands of the demons before the full moon day arrived, and that was for half of the men to stay awake during the night to keep watch while the others slept, and they in turn would sleep during the day while their companions kept watch over them. Although they knew that the demons usually worked during the night, they did not want to risk the chance of their hunger making them turn into demons during the day and devouring them all as they slept.

When the full moon day arrived the men went to the beach to meet the horse. The women followed, crying and begging their men not to leave them. Some held onto the arms of their husbands, refusing to let go, and others held their babies in their arms, pleading with the fathers not to desert their children. The horse arrived and many of the men climbed onto his back, while others, persuaded by their wives, stayed behind, refusing to leave the island.

As the horse flew into the air, the women shouted at their menfolk to come back, and many, still tied by emotional bonds to their women and children, fell from the horse's back, only to find that as they reached the ground the women had turned into demons and were waiting to devour their flesh. In the end only very few men escaped from the island on the back of the horse, and they luckily lived to tell this story and prevent others from being fooled by the beautiful women.

THE PRAYER THAT
WAS ANSWERED

T HE LITTLE ROOM GLITTERED with light from the
butter lamps, arranged neatly on a low table in front
of the shrine. In the light from the lamps one could
pick out the holy objects arranged on the shrine—the sacred
books wrapped in cloth, the image of the Buddha, a framed
picture of the Dalai Lama, silver offering bowls, and on the wall
behind, with incense smoke curling around it, one could see the
thangka painting of Tibet's patron deity and protector, Chenrezik, the bodhisattva of compassion, with eleven heads and a
thousand arms. All around on the walls of the small room were
paintings of other deities, all of whom were objects of devotion
to the people of Tibet. There was a painting depicting Dolma,
the female aspect of compassion, and Jamyang (Manjushri) ,
the bodhisattva of wisdom.

This room, the shrine room, was the richest in the tiny
house, for the people of Tibet were a religious people whose
lives revolved around the teachings of the Buddha, as
expounded by the great gurus and saints who had achieved the
ultimate state of enlightenment. The people believed that
although the great saints had reached the state of enlightenment
they were still concerned for the welfare of all beings, and
remained to protect and guide them on their journey through
this and future lives.

So believed the old woman who sat in the corner of the
shrine room, the beads of her rosary moving through her

fingers as slowly she repeated the prayer of Chenrezik, OM MANI
PADME HUM. Over and over again the powerful prayer rolled
from her lips. The old woman was concerned, for she was a
poor widow, without money or land; all she had in the world
was an only daughter. The old woman knew that without a
dowry to offer, her daughter would not be sought by the rich
men of the land, and so would live her life in poverty and
hunger. The old woman cared not for her own life, for it was
almost over, but she wanted very much for her daughter to be
prosperous and happy. It was for this that she prayed.

Now it happened that a poor man from a neighboring
village had heard of the old woman's daughter, and when he saw
her in the market place he was so moved by her beauty that he
determined to make her his wife. He knew that the mother
would hardly be willing for her daughter to marry a man of such
little substance, so he plotted to make the mother believe that
he was rich and prosperous.

Concealing himself in the shrine room of the old woman's
house, the poor man waited for her to enter, make her offerings
of food, and settle down in the corner to pray. The old woman
prayed and prayed in earnest, begging for a rich man to come and
take her daughter's hand in marriage. The poor man listened and
waited for the old woman to finish; then, just as she was about to
leave the room, he spoke.

The old woman was startled when she heard the voice; seeing
no one in the room she believed it to be the voice of the gods. She
heard the voice say how, in the morning of the next day, a wealthy
man would appear on a white horse, and would ask for her daughter's hand in marriage.

The old woman was overjoyed. With her daughter she
cleaned the house from top to bottom, making it ready for the
rich man the gods were sending as a husband for her daughter.
Then she prepared food and told her neighbors to make ready
for a big celebration the next day, for her only daughter was to
wed a rich man.

The next day the old woman and her daughter awoke early;
the birds were singing and the blue of the sky contrasted with

the fiery mountain peaks, bathed in the glow of the rising sun. The old woman and the daughter were excited and happy, and they settled themselves outside their tiny house to await the arrival of the man on a white horse.

Soon they caught their first glimpse of the man on the horizon. As he rode toward the house the daughter felt sudden pangs of foreboding. She wondered if he would be handsome and kind, and whether her married life would be joyful and happy as she anticipated. All these questions sprang to her mind; then she remembered this man was a gift from the gods so she need feel no fear.

The poor man, dressed in garments his neighbors had lent him, and riding the white horse which was the only one he owned, stopped in front of the old woman's house, dismounted, smiled at the daughter and took her hand in his. The old woman found it hard to contain her excitement and bade the man enter the house to take refreshment. This he did, and after they had talked for a little while he asked the old woman if he could take her daughter's hand in marriage.

There was much joy, a celebration was held, and all the neighbors and friends gathered to wish the couple good fortune, for it was felt that here was a match that was truly made in heaven!

The poor man took the girl, with her few possessions packed in a trunk, and they set off for his humble home in a nearby village. On the journey the poor man began to feel concerned about his deception. He was frightened that the girl would scream and shout when she saw that he was not a rich man at all, but a very humble peasant; he feared too that she would run away and be lost to him forever. The poor man troubled by these thoughts, decided on a plan. He took the girl's possessions out of the trunk and buried them in the earth. Then he ordered the girl into the trunk, telling her that he wished to surprise her when they reached his home. Once the girl was inside the trunk the man locked it and made his way home, leaving the girl in a ditch at the side of a forest path.

When he reached his home the poor man ran to the houses of his nearby neighbors, and telling them that he was bringing home a nervous new bride, warned them not be concerned if they heard screams and shouts during the night. Then he fitted strong new bolts to his door so that the girl would not be able to escape.

While the poor man was away, a rich chieftan passed the spot where the imprisoned girl was lying in the trunk, awaiting the return of her husband. The chieftan ordered his men to open the trunk, and when he saw the girl inside he was so taken by her frail beauty that he took her away with him, leaving a fierce bear in her place inside the trunk.

The poor man returned to fetch his bride, tied a rope around the trunk and dragged it to his home. Inside the house he opened the trunk and was overwhelmed by the fierce bear, made more ferocious by its imprisonment and rough handling. The poor man screamed and shouted for help as the bear attacked him, but the neighbors took no heed of the noise, for they had already been warned.

So the poor man who had plotted and pretended to be a god died at the hands of a savage bear, and the girl lived happily ever after as the wife of a rich chieftan. The old woman's prayers had been answered.

> Whatever happiness is in the world
> Has all arisen from a wish for the
> Welfare of other beings.
>
> Whatever misery there is has arisen
> From indulging in selfishness.

—Buddhist Precepts

THE UMBRELLA TREE

ONCE THERE WAS A MAN named Palden who was a great traveler. He had traveled all around the world and seen many wondrous and glorious sights. One day, while journeying through his homeland of Tibet he came upon a vast forest, and in a clearing in the center of the forest was a huge tree. The tree was very beautiful, with leaves of dark green, which spread like an umbrella over the surrounding land. Feeling tired, Palden decided to rest for a while in the shade of the umbrella tree. Nestling down between the exposed roots of the mighty tree, he was soon asleep.

Suddenly, he woke with a start. It was pitch dark and there was a lot of noise. Very quietly he moved his body so that he could look around the large trunk of the umbrella tree. What he saw made him very frightened, for there in the inky blackness of night were hundreds of eyes, small and shining like the stars of the sky, the eyes of many different animals.

Stealthily, Palden stood up, and very carefully, so as not to disturb the animals, he climbed into the branches of the umbrella tree and looked down on the scene below. An enormous snow lion emerged from the darkness and sat under the tree, quickly followed by a fox, a bear, a monkey, and many other different animals and birds. All the animals and birds that lived in the vicinity of the great forest had sent a representative to the meeting.

The snow lion, who was obviously the leader, looked around at the vast assembly of creatures and said, "Good evening, everybody." And in reply, all the animals chattered and chirped their greetings to the snow lion and each other.

Palden had been so astounded by what he saw that he nearly fell from the branches of the tree when he heard the snow lion speak. Steadying himself on a strong branch he peered wide-eyed at the meeting below.

"Tell me," the snow lion said, "How have you all fared today?"

A wolf replied, "I am very hungry. I have traveled miles today and have not managed to find enough food."

"I have been lucky," said the turtle. "I have enjoyed myself swimming and playing with the frogs."

All the animals related their tales of the day, and as they did so the snow lion made comments, nodded his head in agreement, shook his head in disgust, and every now and then offered some wise advice to the animal concerned.

A silence fell over the meeting and all the animals felt that it was time to return to their territories when a small cough was heard from the back of the crowd. "Excuse me," said a small voice. It was a monkey, very old and shriveled, who stood up and addressed the audience. "I have a sad tale to tell you today. It concerns the stupidity of humans."

"Do tell us," said the snow lion. "What have the humans been up to today."

The monkey continued. "I do wish I was a human," he said. "If I was a human I could do so much to make people happy, but as it is they do not listen to the chatterings of an old monkey."

"Do get on with it," said the fox impatiently, and a rumble of discontent rose in the crowd.

The snow lion raised a paw to silence the crowd, "Let the monkey tell his tale," he said.

"There is a family living by the river," the monkey said. "They have a daughter, an only daughter, and she is very ill. For three months now the girl has suffered from an injury to her leg and the parents do not know how to make it better."

"Now if I was a human," he continued, "I would tell them how to heal their daughter's leg."

All the animals nodded in agreement, indeed they all knew of the stupidity of humans.

The monkey continued with his story. "In front of the house is a huge rock under which lives a frog. The frog is very ill and cannot move for lack of water. Now if the girl's parents were to take that frog, place it on the golden tray from the household shrine and carry it to the river, their daughter's leg would heal very quickly."

The snow lion spoke. "It is true," he said. "The monkey knows the remedy for curing the girl's injured leg, but we have tried to speak with humans before, and they will not listen, they never listen. Now they must find their own way."

After all the animals left, Palden climbed down from the umbrella tree. He was very thoughtful and wondered what he should do.

"The animals have given me guidance," he thought. "I must go and find the family in question and help them to heal their daughter's injured leg."

By the time Palden reached the house the sun had risen in the sky and morning was well advanced. Walking up to the door he knocked loudly. His knock was soon answered by the father, who looked at him questioningly and asked what he wanted.

"I am a doctor," he replied. "I have come to help your daughter."

The father stood aside to let him enter the house and led him to the bed where his daughter was lying, pale and ill, near to death. Palden knelt down beside the bed and took the girl's hand in his own.

"I will make you well again," he whispered. But the girl could not hear him. Palden knew he must hurry if he was to save her life.

Making his way to the outside of the house he found the large rock and gently rolled it a few inches to one side. There sat the frog, dehydrated and dying for lack of water. Palden asked the father to bring him a clean white scarf on the golden tray from the household shrine. Then he very carefully picked up the frog and laid him down on the tray just as the monkey had indicated.

Handing the tray to the father, Palden told him to take the frog to the river and place him in the shallows. "If you do so," he said, "and the frog recovers, your daughter will be well again."

The father did not understand the medicine that this strange doctor was advising, but he had tried everything to cure his daughter, all to no avail, and so he did as the man asked.

When the father returned from the river he was overjoyed to see that his daughter had risen from her bed and was helping her mother to prepare food in the kitchen. Turning to Palden the father said, "Everything I own that is precious is yours; just name what you want, for you have saved our only daughter from death and all the gold in the world could not repay you."

Palden replied, "I want nothing, just to make people happy."

The father insisted that Palden stay and eat with them, and a great feast was prepared in his honor. All the neighbors came to the feast and there was much happiness in the forest that evening, for all believed that a miracle had been performed.

As darkness fell Palden took leave of the family, and carrying gifts that they had heaped upon him he made his way back to the center of the forest, to the clearing in which stood the umbrella tree. By the time he arrived at the tree the meeting was already in progress. All the animals were gathered and were relating their tales of the day to the snow lion. Slowly and quietly, Palden crept up to the tree and climbed into the branches until he was hidden from sight.

This time a tiger was talking about humans, and telling of a family who lived on the far side of the forest, far from the river.

"They are so ignorant," the tiger said, "every day they travel miles to the river to fetch water—it is very difficult."

Once again the animals nodded and grunted knowingly as the tiger continued his story.

"Now if I were them," he said, "I would pull up the old tree stump that stands by their house, dig down for three feet, and there is all the water they could want."

Palden listened, and when the animals had finished he climbed down from the tree. Feeling extremely tired by now, he nestled in between the roots of the tree and fell into a deep sleep but when he awoke he immediately recalled the tiger's tale of the night before. "Was it a dream?" he thought, but when he gazed up into the spreading branches of the umbrella tree he knew that what he had heard was quite true, and that he must find the family who so desperately needed water.

Palden reached the house just as the sun was slipping behind the horizon, but there was still enough light to see the large tree stump. He walked over to inspect it and saw that it was very deeply embedded in the ground. "It will take the strength of fifty men to move this stump," he thought, "so deeply is it rooted in the ground." He sat down by the stump, took some food from inside his chuba, ate, and was soon fast asleep again.

Morning broke. The birds of the forest were singing and sounds of movement from within the house indicated that the family was up and making ready for the day. Palden walked to the front door of the house, knocked, and called to those within to let him enter.

When his call was answered by the woman of the family, Palden asked her to give him some water, but she replied that they had little water for themselves and certainly could not give any away to strangers.

"We have to walk many miles every day," she said, "for we live far from the river and have no other source of water near to home."

"Maybe I can help you," said Palden, "for I am skilled in such matters."

"What do you want?" asked the woman. "If you help us to find water, all that we own is yours."

"All I want," said Palden, "is twenty-five yards of rope and twelve yaks. With these I will bring you all the water you could ever need."

The woman called the rest of her family and together they gathered the yaks and the rope. Palden took the rope, tied it to the tree stump and then to the twelve yaks. Driving the yaks, he made them pull and pull, until at last the stump was lifted from the ground. Then he asked the woman to call all her near neighbors and to ask them to bring shovels with which to dig.

Everyone assembled and took turns digging into the hole left by the tree stump. Before long water began to appear. Clear, fresh spring water filled the hole and overflowed onto the ground.

Everyone cried, laughed, jumped around for joy, hugging each other in their happiness. Suddenly, a voice shouted from the crowd, "Stop!"

Silence fell on the crowd, for the old man who had appeared and shouted the order was very wise and revered among the people. "For sixty-five years," he said, "I have tried to help these people." He turned to Palden. "I have seen their children grow and have children of their own. I have seen many people die, yet neither I nor any other man has been able to do what you have done."

"You are a very special person," the old man continued. "You must be the leader of our people, for you have brought much joy into their hearts, and yet you ask for nothing."

Palden answered, "I will do my best to lead the people of the forest and to make them happy. I thank you for asking me, for I am just a humble man." With this, the crowd lifted Palden onto their shoulders and carried him through the forest proclaiming him their new leader.

After several years had passed and Palden had lived happily among his people, it happened that an old friend of his, hearing of his success, decided to pay a visit to the forest and find out how he had become so famous and well-loved.

Palden welcomed his friend with open arms. "What brings you here, Kunjo?" he asked.

"I wish to know," answered Kunjo, "what made you so successful."

"Oh, it is very simple," replied Palden and he told his friend the story of the umbrella tree and the meetings of the animals.

Now Kunjo listened intently to Palden's story, and thinking that he too would like to be a leader of the people, decided that he would find the umbrella tree and listen to the animals talking. "It will make me very rich and famous," Kunjo thought. "I will have all the gold and silver I desire." And so, that evening, taking leave of Palden, Kunjo made his way to the clearing in the center of the forest and climbed into the branches of the umbrella tree to await the arrival of the animals.

Soon, in the darkness of night, lit only by the pale moonbeams which filtered through the branches of the trees, the animals arrived. Just as the animals were about to start their meeting, a loud crack was heard in the branches of the umbrella tree. The snow lion looked up, and just as he did so, Kunjo fell right at the feet of a large bear. "Ah," said the bear, "so someone is listening to our meeting." He grabbed Kunjo in his powerful arms and hugged him until the breath had left his body and he was dead.

The animals and birds feasted that night and all that was left of poor Kunjo when the sun rose in the morning was a few bones, picked clean of their flesh by the carrion birds.

NOTE: This story, told to us by Yeshe Tsultim, shows how even a comparatively recent tale draws on the Tibetan tradition and its basic assumptions by its emphasis on the inter-relatedness of all things, and the harmony that can be achieved by those who have the wisdom to see the truth. This point is especially well-made when the rescue of the frog restores the girl's health. The frog is a naga who calls for help by affecting the girl. Nagas are spirits whose most widely known form is the snake, a symbol of pure energy and of the beginnings of life. On earth, nagas live as snakes in woods, deserts, and bodies of water. The snake's ability to shed its skin, to be symbolically reborn, is its constructive aspect, while its easily-aroused aggression is the destructive aspect of its nature.

THE NOMAD

by Gyalpo Tsering

He sits and gazes with a song upon his lips
While his yak herds graze: he and they
Are a part of that immense, grassy waste
That stretches desolate where wild winds rage.

All through the day he sings: all else about
Him as if glued to his hoarse voice.
Strange melancholy sails on the sea of grass
At times outsung by the wind's howling song.

At intervals he gathers up his chuba sleeves
To crack his woven sling: at its sound
His shaggy friends throng onward to fresh grass
Coarse, but sweet enough to fill 'til dusk.

Here there are no birds or smell of men
For miles on end, only grazing masses,
Like islands on a calm sea, smeared with colored life,
To welcome a lone traveler, baffled by isolation.

Then, as day wanes and wild winds grow chill,
He gathers the herd with cheerful wolf calls
And shambles behind them, home to the distant tents
That greet and balm the day's toil with rest.

THE LOVERS

ONCE THERE WAS A YOUNG SON in a poor family. He tried to earn a living by scraping what he could from the ground around his home, and by tending to the small herd of yaks that his family owned.

Because he lived on the south side of the river, where the grass was poor and thin, he would often make the long trip across the river, to the north side where the grass was lush and green, and there were hills and valleys where his herd could graze. The journey was many miles, for he had to walk to a shallow place in the river, so that he and his yaks could cross in safety.

It was during one of his frequent trips to the north side that he met a beautiful young girl. She too was tending to her family's herd, but her yaks numbered many more than his, and he knew that she was not poor. Soon, they began to talk to each other. They would relax in the sun while their animals roamed the valley, talking about their lives, their families, their dreams, and hopes for the future. He learned that she had three brothers and that she would take turns with them to tend the herd. Every time he crossed the river, he looked for the girl. Sometimes she was there; sometimes she was not—one of her brothers would be there instead.

Soon, the young couple fell in love. The girl knew that her mother would be very distressed if she learned of their feelings for one another, since the mother hoped her daughter would marry a son of a neighboring family, and it was all but arranged.

So they carried on meeting in secret. Often the boy would sing to her—songs of Tibet, songs of love, songs about the village where he lived. One day he took off one of his long turquoise earrings and gently entwined it in her hair, so that it was hidden. By this they pledged their troth, and as he did this she felt a great sense of sadness, for she knew that her mother would never agree to their union. She sang:

> Tibetan tea is tasty in the mouth,
> Liquor vanishes in the body.
> My beloved darling, our two lives
> Are mingled like the flour in the bowl.

One day, the girl's mother, who had become suspicious of her daughter wanting to go with the herd so often, insisted that she stay at home to bathe and wash her hair. As the girl untied her hair, the turquoise earring fell to her feet and the mother seized upon it.

Flying into an awful rage, she forced the girl to reveal who had given her the earring.

The next day, the mother spoke to her eldest son. "Take this arrow, and when you find this terrible man, kill him." The eldest son took the arrow, but when he came upon the boy he could not bring himself to kill him. Instead he said to the boy, "You run away over the hill, I will shoot a crow and take the bloodstained arrow back to my mother."

This he did, and when the mother saw the arrow she told the son to take it to the village lama. The lama sent the arrow back, with a message that it was a crow's, not human, blood on the arrowhead.

The mother was very angry. She said to the second son, "You take this arrow and kill him." The second son took the arrow, but he too, when he came upon the boy, could not bring himself to kill him. Instead he said to the boy, "You run away

165

over the hill, I will kill a squirrel and take the bloodstained arrow back to my mother."

This he did, and when the mother saw the arrow she instructed the second son to take it once more to the village lama. Back came the message that it was not human blood on the arrowhead.

The mother could contain herself no longer, so deep was her hatred of the boy, and she would not rest until he was dead. She sent for the youngest son, and said to him, "If you kill the man with this arrow I will reward you with gold your father left for me. If you fail to kill him, I will take your life in his place."

The youngest son took the arrow, and when he met the boy he was greatly distressed. He did not wish to kill the boy, but he knew that his own life depended upon it. "If I take the arrow back with human blood on it," he thought, "all will be well, and my mother will think that I have killed the boy. I will shoot him in the leg, and just wound him." He let the arrow fly into the boy's leg, but what he did not know was that his mother had put poison on the arrowhead just before she gave it to him.

He ran and removed the arrowhead from the boy's wounded leg and took it home to his mother. This time the message came back from the lama that it was human blood on the arrowhead. The mother was overjoyed. "At last," she said, "I will be rid of the menace."

The boy suffered in great pain as his leg got worse and the poison went deeper into his body. No longer could he roam with his herd, but he would walk down to the river bank and shout to the girl across the swirling water.

"How is your leg today?" she would shout.

And he would reply, "The pain in my heart is worse by far than the pain in my leg."

The girl fretted and the boy's illness got worse. Then one day she asked him how he was, and he replied, "My love, in this life we will not be together, for I fear that I will surely die this night. If, when you come to the water's edge tomorrow, there is a rainbow in the sky, you will know that I am dead."

The next day she ran down to the water's edge, but long before she got there she saw the rainbow in the sky. She knew that he had died. She sat down on the river bank and cried till her heart was bursting. Then, softly, she heard his voice, coming from nowhere, yet all about her. He was singing.

> The mother river has swollen greatly,
> Do not hinder the water's rushing song;
> When we ourselves have promised,
> No enemy can prevent us.

She walked back to her home, her mother was waiting. She fell down at her mother's feet and wept. She pleaded to be allowed to go to his funeral, and promised that when it was all over she would marry the man of her mother's choosing. Her mother agreed, and together with a maidservant they went to the funeral.

When they arrived, his body was lying on the funeral pyre, but try as they might, the boy's family could not get the body to burn.

The girl took off her robe and threw it onto the boy's body. Immediately, a flame sprang up. She threw her shoes onto the body, and the flame grew higher. Turning to her maidservant, she took the mustard oil that she had brought with her and poured it over her body as she walked into the flaming funeral pyre. The mother looked on horrified as her daughter lay on the burning body of her lover.

When the flames died down, the bones of the couple were molded together. The girl's mother and the boy's mother argued as to how they would separate the remains, so that they could be buried on each side of the river. The girl's mother asked, "What was your son most frightened of in his life?" The boy's mother replied, "Snakes." "My daughter was frightened of frogs," she said.

So a snake and a frog were placed on the bodies, and they separated, the bones moving apart in fear of the animals. The remains were buried on each side of the river, the boy's on the south side, the girl's on the north side.

167

Soon two very large trees grew up in their place, and the branches spread across the river and intertwined. The girl's mother ordered that they be cut down. But shortly afterwards, two bushes grew in place of the trees, and on each sat a little bird. The birds would sing to each other across the river, and fly toward each other, dipping and playing in the cool water.

The girl's mother had the two birds shot, and the bushes pulled up so that no trace of root remained. As the spirits of the two birds flew heavenward, the male bird said to the female, "It seems we are never meant to be together."

"Oh yes we will," replied the female bird. "You go to the salt regions and I will go to the tea regions."

This they did. So, now, whenever you make salty Tibetan butter-tea, the two are joined together.

NOTE: Tibetan tea is made from brick tea, a cake of large black tea leaves, and is churned with butter and salt. This makes quite a nourishing drink; added to tsampa (parched barley flour) it makes a dough-like mixture that is the mainstay of the Tibetan diet.

THE FROG

THE DAWNING SUN'S RAYS flared on the glacier-tipped mountain peaks, surrounding the wide rolling hills which gave way to a valley of patchwork fields. The scene was reflected in the enormous black eyes of a large frog, who sat motionless, save for the occasional blink of an eyelid. His slender body, a full ten inches long, was totally still, and his mottled olive-green skin provided an excellent camouflage among the stones piled at the base of a tall prayer flag pole, beneath which he sat. The frog was intently watching the movements of an old woman as she carefully set light to a pile of juniper branches, their sweet-smelling smoke the same incense rising from countless households throughout Tibet.

Standing just outside the door of her small house on the outskirts of a village, the old lady chanted invocations beside the incense fire, tired lips moving in her tanned, deeply lined face. Her apron, indicating that she was a married woman, was so dust-covered that its rainbow stripes had blurred and faded quite away, as though echoing the many years of her widowhood. While she counted off invocations on her worn wooden rosary, the frog silently hopped over to where she stood. For some moments she did not see him, then, sensing that she was being watched, she turned and was confronted with the unblinking gaze of the large frog. He was, the widow thought, a rather magnificent frog, his skin smoothly stretched over his long limbs, and his black eyes half shaded by overhanging

169

eyelids. The frog gave a loud croak, then slowly, but ever so distinctly, he spoke: "Lady, I have been watching you," he said.

The old woman was astonished, she could not recall ever having heard a frog speak before, and just looked at him in amazement.

He was, the widow thought, a rather magnificent frog. . . .

"I was wondering," the frog continued, "if you would kindly consent to be my mother?" The widow burst out laughing, but rather nervously replied, "How can an animal be my son?"

The frog's throat pouch inflated, he croaked loudly several times, then spoke again: "I am serious," he said, "I would be most grateful if you would agree to be my mother." And so saying, he hopped a little closer so that he was right at the feet of the old woman. The widow was sure this was some sort of joke but did not want to hurt the frog's feelings. She replied that although he was indeed a very fine frog, she could not possibly consent to be his mother. "I am a human being," she said. "You should seek a frog to be your mother."

The frog blinked slowly and continued to gaze at the widow, his eyes like pools of black marble. The widow felt uneasy, and her fingers began to count off the beads on her rosary as she moved her lips in an invocation for protection. It was really a strange request for a frog to make, and the widow began to think that perhaps he was a mischievous spirit. The frog did not move; he just sat at the widow's feet, occasionally croaking, but never removing his gaze from the old woman's face.

"Go away," the widow whispered, "this is no place for a frog; you really must go." The widow noticed how expressive the frog's eyes were, as again he sadly said, "Please, I beg you, be my mother." The widow began to feel anger well up inside her, she shouted at the frog to go away and leave her in peace, not daring to look into his eyes as she spoke, and when she finally did turn again to look at him there was just a glimpse of his back as he hopped with giant leaps onto the pile of stones at the base of the prayer flag, and then disappeared into the distance.

The next afternoon the old woman was sitting on the flat roof of her house busily sorting stock for her stall in the village market. She paused to sip some tea from a silver-lined bowl, and as she lifted the wooden vessel to her lips she became conscious of not being alone. Two large eyes gazed at her, full of impudent confidence. The widow continued to drink her tea while thinking of how to cope with the frog, who was sitting on the edge of the roof, his long legs dangling over the side, one of his forelegs idly scratching his left eyelid. The widow did not acknowledge the frog, but just as she finished her tea the frog repeated his request: "Lady, lady, please be my mother?"

"Kunjosum," she thought, "will he never leave me alone?" "No!" she shouted, "I have told you already. Why do you joke with me?" "Lady, lady," the frog said soothingly, "I am not joking. I really do want you to be my mother." The widow shook her head and walked over to the steep steps leading from the roof, but before she could descend the frog continued, "We could have a very happy life together if you would be my mother."

The widow pleaded with the frog, "I really do not want a frog to be my son; please leave me in peace and go bother someone else."

The frog looked at the old woman with sadness in his eyes, and to her surprise the widow found that his look made her feel guilty. Turning away, she descended the steep wooden steps, leaving the frog where he sat on the flat roof.

All through the next day the old woman busied herself, trying to take her mind off the frog, but still the sight of his deep eyes invaded her thoughts. "He must be a magic frog," she thought, "trying to enchant me."

Very late in the afternoon, as she returned from the river carrying her leather pail of water, the frog hopped up beside her. To her surprise the widow felt glad to see him. "Lady," the frog said as they continued along the empty path, "will you be my mother?" The widow did not reply immediately, but asked herself, as she had done many times that day, what it could mean that the frog sought so persistently to have her as a mother.

"No matter how many times I refuse him, still he comes back," she thought. The deeply tanned face of the widow smiled, creasing her parchment-thin skin. "How much my attitude has changed," she reflected, and it appeared to her from the look in the frog's eyes that he knew her feelings. Had he really enchanted her? Yet she felt no fear, only a warmth of heart. "And if I do become your mother, what will you do as the son of a poor widow?"

"Many things lady, I will do many things for you. Will you be my mother?"

Still worried a little by the situation the widow replied, "Very well, I will be your mother," to which the frog responded by hopping and skipping joyously in front of the old woman toward her little house.

As darkness approached, the widow lit the small mustard lamps with a flint and asked the frog, "Where will you sleep, my son?"

"I will sleep happily in the grate, mother."

With the dawn the old woman awoke and looked across at the frog, who was stretching himself in the warm ash of the clay kitchen stove, and seemed, she thought, very contented. This surprised the old woman, as she thought a wet rock would be a far more suitable bed for a frog.

"Good morning mother, did you sleep well?" the frog inquired.

"Passably," replied the widow as she freshened her face with the cold water from the leather bucket. Then with the worn bellows she brought the yak chips in the brass brazier to life, put the large copper teapot on it to heat, and scooped roasted barley into two plain bowls on the low wooden table. Then she added a little of the thick, buttery tea to the roasted barley. As she put the bowl down in front of the frog, the widow wondered how he was going to manage the meal, and was about to ask him, but already he had sat back on his haunches and was kneading the barley and tea very expertly into a dough.

"Mother," the frog said thoughtfully, "we need some cheese."

"And where will I get cheese, my son?" the widow replied. "I do not have the money to buy any."

"Do not worry, mother," the frog replied, and the widow had the impression he was smiling, "I will get some."

"And how will you carry it? You are far too little."

"I will be able to do it." He spoke with such confidence that the widow could not help but laugh, and as the frog was anxious to depart she gave him her blessing.

"All right, be on your way; may Chenrezik protect you and may you find your cheese." She watched from the doorway as with great eager hops the frog set off toward the market place.

Hidden by a large bush, the frog looked out into the busy market place. He was soon covered in the dust kicked up by the yaks, mules, and horses of the merchants who were loading their pack animals and making ready to depart from the local inn. Crowds milled around the stalls, and the frog left the shelter of the bush and began to wander around until he found exactly what he was looking for. Without hesitation he leaped straight onto the back of a mule laden with sacks of cheese. The mule shied as the frog landed on his back, but settled down at

his firm command. Villagers shouted in disbelief at the sight of
the frog on the mule, and soon a crowd gathered, but no one did
anything to remove the frog or stop the mule trotting through
the village with the frog, apparently in complete control, balanced on its back! Everyone agreed that a mule being ridden by
a frog was too strange an occurrence to be interfered with, and
the villagers argued among themselves as to whether it was
auspicious or not, with the majority of them convinced that it
was some mischievous demon.

As the widow heard the mule outside she rushed to open
the door, and saw that the frog had indeed brought home a
plentiful supply of cheese! Even as they were eating the cheese,
after unloading and storing the large sacks, the widow did not
believe it! "But you cannot have done it all by yourself. I do not
believe it!"

The frog laughed, "Is it any more surprising than my being
your son?"

Said the widow thoughtfully, "You are indeed my son, and
as you are my son I should know who you are."

The frog just croaked and chuckled.

"You are not human," the widow said, "yet, nor are you a
frog; you are something special." But the frog did not answer;
he just gave a wistful smile.

The following day, after they had eaten their breakfast, the
frog announced that he had another idea. The old woman
laughed, "What is it this time?"

"Mother, what I need now is a wife," the frog answered.
For a moment the widow was filled with sadness, she could not
imagine any female frog enjoying the life that her son now led,
and she knew enough of life to know that the frog could not
deny his wife the life that she would surely want.

"Alright my son," the widow smiled, "you must do what
you want, but be sure to choose your wife with care." So
bidding his mother farewell, the frog began his adventure,
hopping through the door into the sunlight.

As the days passed the widow became concerned, and she
began to wonder if she had been right in letting the frog go to

seek a wife. She began to reflect on all the things that could have happened to him, a small frog, alone in the world, prey to many wild animals—he could even now be dead. The widow waited, many days passed, but still no sign of the frog. She went about her work with a heavy heart, and realized just how deep her feelings were for her newly acquired "son."

The frog, however, had no intention of marrying a frog, and visited all the houses in the neighborhood where he knew there was an unmarried daughter. But after carefully assessing the potential candidates he was not impressed with any of the likely brides. Then, on the morning of the fourth day, he peeped through a rice-paper window into a fine house owned by a merchant. The frog had heard about the merchant's lovely daughter, and by the end of the morning, after watching the girl, he knew that he had found the one he would take for his wife. Now, only the arrangements were to be made, and the frog felt very happy. He went in search of the girl's father, and when he found him the frog hopped up onto one of the carpet-covered seats that lined the room where the merchant was changing his clothes. The merchant's usual worried expression intensified when he saw the frog. "How did you get here?" he said to himself, looking at the frog and pulling on his knee-length appliqued felt boots. To the merchant's astonishment the frog replied to the question.

"By hopping, and sometimes I walked."

"Who are you?" the merchant asked, gripping the hilt of his sword, "and what are you?"

"I am just a frog who has come to see you and to talk to you." The melodious voice of the frog had a soothing quality so the merchant's fear and aggression melted away. Even so, he remained very cautious and puzzled as he asked, "Who are you? You must be king of the frogs." He pulled on his grey chuba, leaving one sleeve loose.

The frog spoke. "I have come," he said in a voice full of confidence, "to ask for your daughter as my wife."

The merchant angrily picked up his woven belt and knotted it around his waist, pulling his chuba up so that it was knee-length, according to the custom of East Tibet. "I do not know what you are, frog," he said, "whether you are demon or spirit, but whatever you are, you cannot marry my daughter." Desperately the merchant was wondering how he could get a message to his brother, a lama who would know how to beat this frog-demon.

The frog realized that the merchant was not going to be easily persuaded; he had to admit that most parents would need a lot of convincing to allow their daughter to marry a frog! "If you will not let your daughter marry me," the frog replied, "I will cough."

The merchant thought that a cough did not really require an announcement. "Go ahead and cough," he said to the frog.

It seemed to the merchant that the frog smiled, then he drew in his breath sharply, and coughed, or the merchant supposed he coughed. But from the depths of the frog's throat came a thunderous roar which beat the merchant to the ground and shook the whole house. As the merchant staggered to his feet he drew his sword, intending to kill the frog. The animal fixed him with his black eyes and coughed again, just as the merchant was about to bring the sword slicing down onto the frog's back. The roar filled the air, the room cracked, furniture split, crockery fell onto the floor. The merchant's sword cracked and fell apart, and his house was devastated. The door burst open and the merchant's wife ran in, terrified. The merchant answered her question before she asked it.

"He coughed," the merchant said, pointing to the frog. "Please," he said, "we will let you marry our daughter, no more coughing, I beg you!"

The merchant's wife wept at her husband's words, then both of them looked in horrified anticipation as the frog drew in his breath, but instead of a loud roar, there came instead a gentle sigh, like refreshing breeze, and for a moment they both felt soothed and caressed.

"Look!" The merchant's wife felt the wall which had cracked with the almighty coughing of the frog. "Look!" she repeated, amazed as her hand ran over the smooth wall; the crack healed as thought it had never been! The merchant and his wife saw that at the moment of the frog's sigh, everything in their home that had been broken or damaged was restored to its former condition.

The merchant's wife sat down heavily on one of the low rug-covered seats in the small room. She was dressed in a brocade chuba, with a large coral-studded silver milk-pail hook hanging from her waist. Nervously she fingered the star-shaped turquoise reliquary hanging around her neck. She pleaded with her husband, trying to reason with him. Had he gone quite mad? "How can our daughter marry a frog?"

The frog hopped onto a bench opposite the couple and, looking large and squat, spoke to the merchant and his wife in a voice full of the melody of music, clear and precise, like the breaking of an icicle. It was indeed a strange voice, and the couple felt compelled to listen. "Human beings, animals, birds, even frogs, we are all of the same spiritual force, so do not worry."

"Perhaps," the merchant's wife thought. "Divine beings and saints can see we are all one." But to her eyes there and then, they were far from being the same, and she could not reconcile herself with the fact that all beings were the same under the skin.

"We know you are a very special frog," the merchant said, "but you are asking for our only daughter, to take her away with you; we may never see her again." He stood in front of the frog, and again thought what a curious charm there was about him, even when he was silent, tentatively listening.

"You will not lose your daughter," the frog said. "She will have everything she desires."

The merchant's wife looked at the frog with pleading eyes, and the frog could see the glistening of tears ready to overflow down her cheeks. "Anything else!" she cried, "We will give you our house, our wealth, all you could want, but please, not our precious only daughter!"

But the frog replied, "If you do not give me your daughter, I will cry." He looked so sad that the girl's mother felt a wave of

177

compassion rise in her breast. Just as the frog finished speaking two tears welled up from his eyes, and the horrified parents looked on as the tears became a rushing torrent which quickly filled the house and the surrounding land, as if each teardrop was an ocean. The couple jumped onto a chest that was floating by and as it reached the steep stairway to the flat roof, they climbed off and made their way to the roof where the rest of the household was already waiting. The frog followed them, tears still streaming from his eyes.

"Please stop crying," shouted the merchant, as his servants looked on in amazement. The merchant's wife wailed as she saw all the barley, flour, and their best clothes float out of the house. "Please stop crying," she said. "Stop and you may marry our daughter."

The frog croaked and stopped crying, and just as soon as the water had evaporated from his skin, all the water in the house and the surrounding countryside dried up. Clothes, flour, and grain were all dry as if never touched by the torrential water, and before the wife's invocation to Chenrezik had passed her lips. The merchant and his wife watched their servants collect their belongings and furniture and return them to the house. The frog noticed a tree in which a fox, a chicken, and a cat had taken refuge, fear of water creating harmony among these naturally antagonistic animals. He looked at the merchant expectantly, but the merchant's face was creased with anxiety. His wife tried to explain that they could not let their daughter marry a frog.

"We would be ashamed," she said. "How could she live and say that she is married to a frog?"

"It is not necessary," said the frog, "for you to worry. Can you not see that all beings, human or animal, are the same?"

But they did not see, and the frog could see in their eyes what they could not bring themselves to say—that they thought a frog was one of the lowliest of beings, and not even a special frog such as himself was any more worthy of their daughter's hand.

The merchant ordered one of his servants to bring a large
metal-bound trunk onto the roof. "Look," he said to the frog,
producing a large key and opening the trunk, revealing a mound
of silver hooves. "Please take these with you."

The frog croaked and laughed. The girl's parents were
alarmed, but they said, "You cannot have our daughter, but
you laugh."

The frog looked disdainfully at the treasure. "It is not your
treasure I want," he said, "but your daughter." The frog
laughed heartily, and as he did so, flames sprang up all over the
house and began to consume the building. None of the servants'
attempts to suffocate the flames could make any impression on
the fire. "Please, you are destroying our house!" The servants,
the merchant, and his wife all shouted in unison. The frog
laughed even louder and the flames grew more intense. "You
shall have our daughter," the merchant and his wife cried. "You
are indeed a special frog, our daughter *will* be your wife." The
frog croaked, and as he stopped laughing the flames subsided.
Everything that had been burning so fiercely was unscathed.

*The frog laughed heartily, and as he did so, flames sprang up all over the
house and began to consume the building.*

179

While the merchant and his wife went to tell their daughter of her fate, the frog softly sang with the wind that caressed the prayer flags hanging at a corner of the roof. When the frog saw the merchant's daughter again, he thought that she was indeed a great beauty, with pale skin and delicate features framed in jet black cascading hair. Her eyes reflected a quick mind and her voice was sweet and gentle. She smiled politely at the frog, but without any warmth, and he saw that her heart was full of unhappiness.

"We must prepare to leave for my home," he said. "It is not far. I think you will like it." As the girl quickly turned away to hide her tears the frog continued. "Remember what I say, and try to understand that I can make you very happy. Remember that we are all one." But the girl could not reply. She looked at him for a few moments and wondered despairingly how she could live a life married to a frog. No matter how nice, still, a frog!

The frog went to refresh himself at the stream, happily swimming among the water plants and hopping from rock to rock, while his young bride prepared for her journey. She wept as her mother helped pack her clothes and belongings into brass-bound wooden traveling chests.

"Listen to me, Choden-la." Her father took her aside, wiping away her tears with his handkerchief. "You must be very brave." He gripped her shoulders.

"Yes Pa-la. I will try. But a frog . . . What will become of me?" Her eyes filled with tears of despair.

"Listen to me; there is a chance." Her father's voice was low and hurried, as though he feared the frog, with his extraordinary powers, would overhear him. "On the journey to his home you will have a chance." Choden looked at him expectantly, puzzled. "You must kill him. Then you will be free." The girl shook her head vigorously. "You must, my daughter!" He is some kind of demon, I am convinced of it. You have to be free of him."

"But how could I kill him? He would soon know of my plans," the girl said to her father. "You have seen his powers."

From a cupboard decorated with intricately painted flowers, her father took three leather pouches, saying "You will not need any weapon to kill the frog . . . ." "But how Pa-la?" the girl asked again with a note of desperation in her voice. He gave her the three leather pouches. "Put these carefully inside your chuba. One pouch contains hooves of turquoise, another hooves of silver, and the third hooves of gold. During your journey strike the frog on the head with one of these. It is no good using an ordinary rock; it would have no effect against a demon. But one of these substances will kill the frog and give you your freedom."

"I will try Pa-la," the girl said sadly.

A few hours later the frog and his bride began their journey. Choden's luggage had been strapped to two pack mules, and the frog led her fine horse. She was amazed by the speed of the frog and the distance they covered. He never seemed to tire, yet she thought hopping must be a very wearisome way to get around. For some time they traveled in silence. Choden became increasingly aware of the silence. It was emphasized by the clink of the horse's and mule's hooves on stone, and their breath, harsh from exertion; these were the only sounds in the vast stony plain that they had entered. In the far distance rose snowcapped peaks and dominating, encompassing all, was the turquoise sky. It was, the girl thought, the silence of the sky. She knew that pilgrims traveling to the holy places had been aware of this silence, a tangible silence, a presence, some said, of the gods.

After they had been traveling for many hours, Choden realized she must overcome her fear and kill him soon if she was to escape the frog. Already they were very far from her parents' house. As the sun sank behind the mountains and the shadows lengthened she carefully took the largest lump of turquoise from the leather pouch in her chuba. She was very frightened but with all her strength she hurled it at the frog, who was only a few feet ahead of her. It struck him sharply on the head, but to her horror bounced right off. The frog appeared not to feel anything, but caught sight of the turquoise and hopped over to pick it up. He held it up to the girl. Surely this demon will punish me, she thought, but she saw only laughter in his dark expressive eyes. "You must have dropped this. Take care of it." She took the turquoise from him with murmured thanks and they continued on their way. She felt thoroughly confused and frightened.

It was another full-day's journey before Choden could summon up enough courage to try and kill the frog again. This time she chose a hoof of silver. She had heard of many demons and ghosts successfully chased away with ritual weapons of silver. She decided not to throw it, but edged her horse up closer to the frog, then with all her strength brought the sharp lump of silver down on his head. It felt as thought it had struck iron, and with the impact of the blow the silver flew from her hand, and an intense pain shot up her arm, but the frog, to her astonishment, did not appear to have felt the slightest touch. There was not a moment's hesitation in his rapid steady hops.

His young wife was now very frightened indeed and to her horror the frog suddenly stopped, glanced back, and saw the piece of silver. Again he carefully recovered the treasure and handed it back to his wife. "You may need this one day." He spoke quietly, but she could not look into his eyes and her face was flushed with embarrassment and guilt. Now she decided that there really was nothing to be done and she must be thankful that the frog had only responded kindly. In fact, she thought, it is such a shame that he is a frog, as he really seems very nice and kind. But still he is a frog, even if apparently a magic one.

As they traveled the girl wondered what life would be like with her new husband. Where would they live? It surely could not be in the world of men, this home he talks of, for there was no place for a frog, even a magic frog, in the world of men. She tried to remember what type of homes frogs usually had, and could only think of dank and murky water. But somehow, she felt that this frog, being no ordinary frog, was more likely to live in one of the heavens, or, she thought, perhaps one of the hells!

Neither did she look forward to, for she found the world still a lovely and exciting place, and was sure she would have little in common with gods. Finally, in desperation, Choden decided she had to try the gold against the frog. Was it not the very metal of the gods—symbol of everything holy? She took the largest hoof of gold from her bag. Carefully she waited until the horse was close enough to the frog, then closing her eyes, she used both hands to bring the gold crashing down on his head. Surely this time, she thought, I will have killed him. The gold felt as though it had struck a cloud. Her eyes opened. "Have I missed? No!" She seemed to lose her grip on the lump of gold in a thick cloud, and the frog, unperturbed, hopped on. Choden silently began to cry. Then she realized that her horse had stopped. She wiped her eyes and looked down at the frog.

His voice was gentle and she realized how loving it sounded. "Here, I have found what you lost." He gave her the piece of gold. "You must stop losing your treasure," he said with a laugh so pleasant and infectious that his young wife smiled in response and began to feel at ease in his company. Indeed, when she thought about it her tears had been tears of relief as much as anything and she was very glad she had not harmed him. To harm a frog with such a loving nature could not be good. Perhaps, she told herself, life will be better than I imagine.

"Mother! Mother! Please open the door." The widow could not believe that the frog had returned; she wept with happiness as she opened to the door to greet her "son." The widow was astounded to see that the frog clearly had been successful in his search for a wife, far beyond the imagination of the widow. His bride was beautiful with, the widow thought, eyes that were alight with love; she must indeed be a fairy.

The frog's home was not at all what his bride had expected. Although it was far humbler than that of her parents, still it was a very warm and loving place and Choden realized, to her surprise, that she was happy. That night the three of them celebrated and talked. The frog told the widow of his adven-

183

tures, and his "mother" told them how for many days people
from all parts of the district, even the most distant valleys, had
traveled to their village to take part in the horse races. Almost
all the villagers were camped by the river in picnic tents, and
tomorrow the races would begin.

Early on the following day, the frog, his bride, and
"mother" prepared to watch the first day of the horse races. The
frog said he had some things to do, and so he would like the two
women to go on ahead of him to the festival ground, and he
would join them later. Choden and the widow were surprised,
but went to the festivities, leaving the frog alone in the house.
He watched them through a tiny hole he made in the rice-paper
window, until they were out of sight. For a few moments the
frog sat thoughtfully in the middle of the room, then inflated
his throat pouch, croaked, and in a moment was transformed
into a handsome young man, the only sign of his previous form
the frog skin lying crumpled at his feet. Carefully, he took some
salt out of a box and sprinkled it over the skin, which he then
hung on a hook in a dark corner.

In the stable there were two horses belonging to the
widow. He took the best hoping that with her poor eyesight she
would not recognize it at the races. At the festival, large decorated tents surrounded the race track, and much of the day was
spent in singing, dancing, feasting, and playing mah jong. But
everything stopped when a race was to be run. During the races,
the competitors had to perform feats of skill, such as firing an
arrow at a moving target, picking up a scarf from the ground
with their teeth, or fighting their way past a dummy opponent
with a sword.

The days of the festival passed very pleasantly and gradually one rider clearly emerged as the champion, but he was a
mystery to everyone. No one seemed to know who he was or
where he came from, and he could never be found after the
races. Such was his skill and such was the mystery surrounding
him that he was rumored to be one of the gods. But the frog's
wife increasingly felt, when she saw the handsome young man,
that she knew him. At different times during the festival the

frog was with them and once or twice she had mentioned her feeling about the young man to him, but the frog had just laughed.

On the fifth day of the festival, Choden made a secret plan. Again the handsome young man was competing in the race and this time before it was finished she ran as fast as she could back to the widow's house. As usual the frog had said that he would follow later, but he still had not come to the festival ground. When his wife called out for him, there was no response. Carefully the girl searched the house, but there was no sign of the frog. Something hanging on a hook in the shadows caught her eye and when she held it up she realized it was a frog's skin. Now she really knew who the young man was!

For a moment Choden hesitated, but then, using the bellows on the brass brazier, she worked the smoldering yak chips into glowing embers, bundled up the frog skin and consigned it to the fire. As the last fragment was burned she heard footsteps outside the door and quickly hid in a dark corner. The handsome young man entered and promptly went to the hook where he had hung the skin, but even as he stepped over to it he realized the skin was gone. As he looked about the room for it, his wife felt his dark eyes piercing the gloom as they caught sight of her.

"Husband," she stepped from the shadows, "I have burned the frog skin." Even she now began to realize the magnitude of what she had done. At first the young man looked infinitely sad. His magic was gone. No longer could he continue his work.

"I cannot change back now. I am trapped here."

"I am glad," his wife said. "I knew it was you at the races, that was why I came back early, before you would have time to change back into a frog."

As time passed the young man's love for his wife grew so that he was glad to remain in the world of mankind. He knew that many would tell his story and so learn that all things differ only in their "skin," their form, and that all are really of one nature.

NOTE: Another story, like "The White Rooster" and "The Castle in the Lake," of the release of a person from an animal form. These stories reflect man's spiritual struggle toward transformation into full humanity. The frog, seen as rising from the waters of creation, is a symbol of rebirth or renewal in many cultures.

186